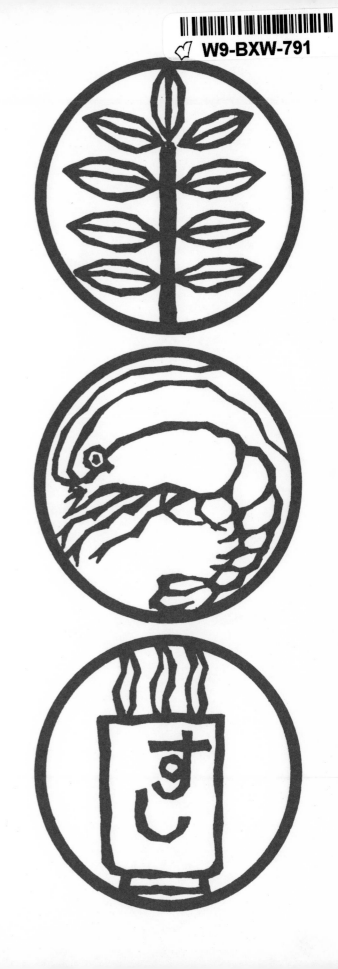

SUSHI AT HOME

SUSHI AT HOME

Edited by Kay Shimizu

SHUFUNOTOMO / JAPAN PUBLICATIONS

First printing, 1988

© Copyright in Japan 1988 by Shufunotomo Co., Ltd.
Illustrations by An Corporation
Photographs by Shufunotomo Co., Ltd.

Front Cover:
Recipe by Michiko Ubukata
"Shikki" Japanese Laquerware:
Omukai Ko-Shu-Do Co., Ltd. Tokyo.

Back Cover:
Recipes by Ai Kidosaki

Photographs by Shufunotomo Co., Ltd.
Cover design by Momoyo Nishimura

Recipes by
Doi, Masaru (pages 21, 34), Iida, Miyuki (pages 48, 82), Egami, Eiko (page 100), Fujita, Fuki (page 32),
Ohmae, Kinjiro (pages 32, 33), Kaneda, Mikiko (page 30), Kohno, Sadako (pages 37, 86), Makita, Fumiko
(pages 108, 126), Shimizu, Kay (pages 116, 118, 120, 122), Suzuki, Tokiko (pages 22, 62, 77, 78, 110, 129),
Tsutsui, Taiko (page 70), Ubukata, Michiko (pages 93, 94), Yamaguchi, Aiko (pages 38, 40, 60, 84, 96, 98,
111, 112, 113), Yamamoto, Mitsuo (page 115), Shufunotomo Co., Ltd. (pages 26, 51, 56, 74, 81, 88, 104,
114, 132)

Published by SHUFUNOTOMO CO., LTD.
2-9, Kanda Surugadai, Chiyoda-ku, Tokyo, 101 Japan

Overseas Distributors: Japan Publications Trading Co., Ltd.
P.O. Box 5030, Tokyo International, Tokyo, Japan

Distributors :
UNITED STATES : Kodansha International/USA, Ltd., through
Harper & Row, Publishers, Inc., 10 East 53rd Street, New York,
New York 10022. Canada : Fitzhenry & Whiteside Ltd.,
195 Allstate Parkway, Markham, Ontario L3R 4T8.

ISBN : 0-87040-767-8   LC : 88-080144
Printed in Japan

PREFACE

Since *sushi* making is an entirely different approach from any other type of food preparation it cannot be stressed enough that you familiarize yourself with the entire book contents first before attempting these recipes. Read the tips, the recipe methods, understand the ingredients, study the glossary and save yourself much energy later wondering about this or that. You might begin by practicing how to properly prepare rice as your first lesson. This volume incorporates many authors' ideas so there will be varied methods to prepare similar ingredients.

These *sushi* recipes basically serve four but yield depends upon appetites! So experiment flamboyantly and yours will become a dazzling new experience. All recipes in this book indicate usage of raw rice to prepare the vinegared rice (*shari*). If cooked prepared vinegared rice (*shari*) is required it will so state.

Raw fish when very fresh is not fishy smelling or ill tasting. It practically melts in your mouth and there are many persons who savor delicate raw fish as their favorite instead of a formerly favored beef steak! The combination with vinegared seasoned rice to form *sushi* is fabulous!

SUSHI AT HOME will introduce you to the joys of *sushi*—a delectable gourmet experience.

Acknowledgments with thanks go to Shufunotomo Company Managers A. Gohara and K. Nagai and staff who agreed to publish this material. To Editor Michiko Kinoshita for her enduring devotion to her work, to the many Japanese authors who gave permission for their recipes to be the basis for the composition of this book. Recipes by Masaru Doi, Miyuki Iida, Eiko Egami, Fuki Fujita. Kinjiro Ohmae, Mikiko Kaneda, Sadako Kohno, Fumiko Makita, Kay Shimizu, Tokiko Suzuki, Taiko Tsutsui, Michiko Ubukata, Aiko Yamaguchi. And to Noriko Matsuda for her translation assistance.

CONTENTS

Metric Conversion Table

1 oz. = 28 grams
1 lb. = 0.45 kg
1 tsp. = 5 ml
1 Tbsp. = 15 ml
1 fluid oz. = 30 ml
1 cup = 0.24 liters
1 inch = 2.5 cm

INTRODUCTION

Sushi at last has become very popular and spreading worldwide to a rightful position. And the sophisticated palate of the *sushi* enthusiast is being satisfied even at the expense of his pocketbook. *Sushi* dishes are based on seasoned vinegared rice garnished, mixed, rolled, pressed or tossed with assorted ingredients.

You can sit at a *sushi* bar, relax, use the hot steamy *o-shibori* (hand towel usually rolled tightly like a fat cigar) to refresh yourself as well as cleanse your hands. The warm congeniality and conversation of the Master Chef and his several assistants envelops you immediately. There is a glassed-in refrigerated display in front of the customer. Pointing to whatever you desire the *sushi* is prepared quickly by the deft hands of the Masters. This *sushi* is usually *nigiri-zushi*—formed by the Chef's hands compressing the vinegared flavored rice into a small oval topped with slices of fresh raw fish, omelet, squid or what is your desire served in pairs.

The room temperature vinegared rice unites the flavors magically with the various types of fresh fish toppings or whatever you choose. One dips the end of the *sushi* topping into a small dish of light *shoyu* (Japanese soy sauce) and enjoys the taste delight. Condiments such as thinly sliced sweet vinegared ginger are eaten either with chopsticks or fingers. This spicy interruption in between courses helps to clear the palate for the *sushi* "rapture." Plenty of hot green tea (with no sugar or cream) in tall cups without handles is a part of the *sushi* ritual. Or you can order warm *saké* (Japanese rice wine) or refreshing Japanese beer famed worldwide.

Green *shiso* (beefsteak plant) and *kinomé* (an aromatic herb—prickly ash) are often used for bright edible garnishes, if available. They add piquant flavor while eating *sushi*. The attractive color pictures in this volume will offer an assortment of possible garnishes both edible and decorative for inspiring you to imitate the recipes at hand. You can of course make your substitutions but plan to use garnishes which will be subtle and complement the *sushi* flavors.

The authentic *sushi* chef expertise takes years of apprenticeship and few of us could ever hope to match a *sushi* bar atmosphere. But we can now enjoy making *sushi* in its many different forms in our homes. (Although many Japanese housewives send out for *sushi* much as Americans send out for pizza).

This book is a treasury of expertly authored Japanese recipes which I have edited, rewritten and adapted for use by Westerners who love the intriguing Japanese food called *sushi*. Also included are *sushi* recipes . . . Western-style . . . of my own which I have used in teaching Asian food classes in California.

People have learned the Japanese flavors of *teriyaki, sukiyaki, tempura, yakitori, sashimi*, etc. and are now ready for the most sophisticated taste of all—*Sushi*! Saying *o-sushi* gives the honorific term of "o" to the *sushi* noun. Certainly *sushi* deserves this honor. When an adjective is in front of the noun there is a slight change in phonetics. *Sushi* in this instance becomes *zushi*.

Precision of measurement . . . simplicity of ingredients . . . use of the impeccably freshest and the best in the market place are the most important features in the preparation of any Japanese food especially *sushi*! Seasonal availability and visual aesthetic beauty are foremost. It is not a cuisine that the most is the best. In fact Japanese foods could be categorized as the least is the most fulfilling since visual pleasure is as essential as the consumption of the healthful food itself.

Enjoy this new gastronomical adventure!

Kay Shimizu, Editor
Author of Asian Cookbooks

About the Editor:
Kay Shimizu is a Japanese-American who has 35 years of Asian foods teaching and writing experience in the United States. Her cookbooks published by Shufunotomo Company, Tokyo, Japan are as follows:
    Asian Cookbook for Beginners
    Weight Control with Asian Foods
    Gourmet Wok Cooking
    Japanese Foods for Health
    Cooking with Exotic Mushrooms

HISTORY OF *SUSHI*

Sushi in Japanese literature dates back to the *Heian* period (AD 794–1185). The concept of *sushi* in those ancient days was different from the present day. Rice was not used. Fish and clams were pickled with salt and a sour taste developed. In the 17th Century rice was added to the pickled fish to ferment rapidly producing lactic acid. And the rice was discarded except for some grains which stuck to the fish. The tart taste experience was delicious and good. But it was time consuming as well as expensive.

Thereafter instant vinegared rice replaced the fermented rice. Vinegared rice (*sushi*) in the present style dates back to the middle of the *Edo* period (A.D. 1700). Expensive foods were forbidden during the *Tempo* Reformation (A.D. 1841–1843). Vinegared rice with gizzard shad, vinegared rice wrapped in fried soybean cake and vinegared rice with *nori* seaweed became widely popular since they were cheap, tasty and utilized readily available ingredients. Each regional area developed its own *sushi* specialty depending upon its distinctive local products.

Since the country of Japan is surrounded by water there is an abundance of fresh seafoods in most localities. Today we can delight in even a more varied *sushi* assortment whether we live in Japan or in another country. With modern refrigeration, preservation and airfreight methods freshness is not a great problem as is the past.

As you prepare the many *sushi* recipes in this marvelously photographed SUSHI AT HOME cookbook you will note that there is a variance in the sourness, the sweetness, the saltiness and much more *sushi* variety than you ever imagined. These can be adapted to your own tastes. Depending upon the temperature of the rice and the topping/mixture some flavors stand out more than the others.

▶

Top Right: *Sushi Teishoku*
Top Left: *Sushi Kaiseki*
Middle: *Chakin-Zushi*
Bottom Right: Rolled *Sushi*
Bottom Left: *Oshi-Zushi*

NUTRITIONAL VALUE OF *SUSHI*

The traditional Japanese diet uses very little animal fat and seafood is favored over meat. Nutritionally *sushi* with fish is fairly low calories plus excellent protein, unsaturated fats and vitamins. Fish is easier to digest. Seaweed (sea vegetable) has fabulous potential containing protein, vitamins and minerals essential to good health. Rice has only 100 calories per 100 grams (3½ oz.). *Sushi* with its use of seaweed, fish and other marine products along with rice furnishes a natural well balanced combination for physical well being.

THE LANGUAGE OF *SUSHI*

Special colorful terms are used only in the *sushi* shop vocabulary. Here are a few examples of this very interesting tradition.

Agari: A large cup of green tea. Literally means completed. *O-agari* is polite form.

Gari: The light pink slightly sweet pickled ginger slices (*amazu shoga*) served with *sushi* to be munched on between the various *sushi* courses.

Géso: Octopus—refers to the legs.

Gyoku: Rolled egg omelet (*tamagomaki*) means jewel.

Hikari mono: Fish with scales removed leaving the skin intact with its glossy appearance shiny.

Himo: The edge of the ark shell clam.

Itamaé-san: *Sushi* chef.

Kappa: Cucumber.

Kataomoi: Sea Urchin.

Kusa: Seaweed.

Murasaki: *Shoyu* (Japanese soy sauce).

Namida: Refers to *wasabi* (Japanese horseradish) which often causes you to cry from the spicy hot flavor. Literally means tears.

Nami no hana: Salt in this case called romantically "Flowers of the waves." In ancient days seawater furnished the salt directly without being processed.

Odori-ebi: Shrimp is served alive so it "dances" before your eyes and one eats it while it wiggles in your mouth! Sweet flavor—almost unexplainably delicious.

Otémoto: Chopsticks (*hashi*).

Sabi: *Wasabi*—potent and spicy Japanese green horseradish.

Sabi-nuki: No *wasabi* please.

Shari: The basic vinegared seasoned *sushi* rice for preparing the assorted varieties of *sushi*.

Sugata-zuke: A small whole fish topping a *nigiri zushi*.

Tama: Ark shell.

Témaki: Hand rolled small *sushi* either like an ice cream cone shape or vertically rolled.

Téppo-maki: *Sushi* made by wrapping with *nori* seaweed and *kanpyo* (gourd shavings).

Yunomi: Large tea cups such as used in *sushi* shops without handles.

EQUIPMENT & UTENSILS

Equipment and Utensils for Making *Sushi*:

Wooden bowl for mixing:
* A wooden rice tub for preparing vinegared rice (*shari*) is ideal. A flat wooden platter or unseasoned, unvarnished shallow wooden salad bowl (previously not used for salad making to be saved exclusively for *sushi*) should be porous enough to absorb the excess moisture of the *sushi* rice while being prepared. There is a special Japanese cedar container called a *handai*. It is very expensive and not necessary for preparation of *sushi* although nice to own.
* Wipe the wooden platter or bowl with a cloth moistened with the vinegar/water solution (*tezu*) see below.

Fan:
* A large fan (manual or electric) to "breeze away" the heat to quickly cool the rice. The quicker this vaporizing is accomplished the more lustrous the rice grains will glow while the mixture cools to room temperature at the same time.

Shamoji (wooden rice paddle):
* Rice paddle made from bamboo is used for tossing the rice kernels and for serving. It is flat in the paddle area—not cupped like a spoon. Rinse with cold water first (shake off the excess) before using to toss the rice. This will prevent the rice from sticking to the paddle. When making *sushi* you can use the vinegar/water solution as a dip for the paddle.

Sudaré (bamboo rolling mat):
* This is a bamboo mat similar to a small place mat. It is made from skewer type bamboo sticks woven together with string and is used for making rolled sushi (*maki-zushi/norimaki*). A good substitute would be a flexible place mat. Do not wet the *sudaré* prior to use. Keep dry. After use clean *sudaré* by hand and dry promptly so the water and detergent will not soak into the slats and string.

Cloth and *tezu*:
* A cotton cloth is best since it rinses and drains well. Linen is also suitable. The dry cloth is used for the vinegared rice wrapped in *nori* (*maki-zushi/norimaki*). A dampened cloth is used for press forming vinegared rice with pickled mackerel, etc. and a special shape is desired.
* *Tezu* (water mixed with rice vinegar—*su*) or *sumizu*
    1 cup water
    2 tablespoons rice vinegar (*su*)
    1 teaspoon salt
Dampen the fingers with this *tezu* mixture so that the vinegared rice
(*shari*) does not stick to your hands/fingers and equipment.

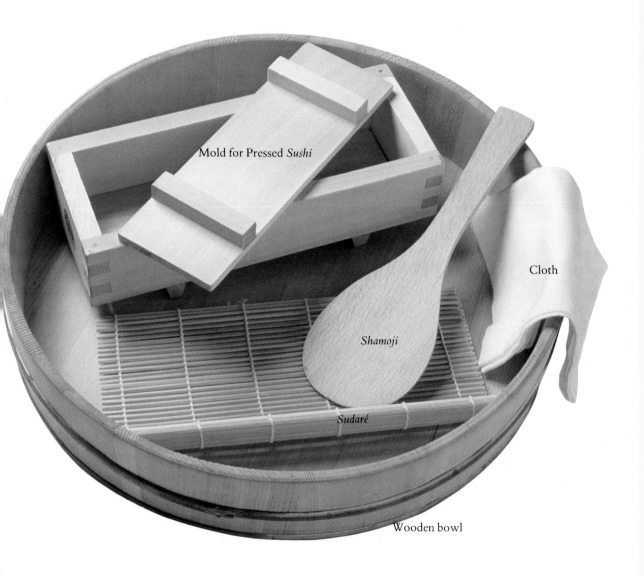

Mold for Pressed *Sushi*

Cloth

Shamoji

Sudaré

Wooden bowl

Warning:
Using only water on your hands to prepare *nigiri-zushi*, etc. could spoil the *sushi*. The vinegar helps to preserve the rice. This vinegar/water solution can also be used for dampening the wooden rice paddle, sealing the *nori* (laver seaweed) in *maki-zushi/norimaki* preparation, wetting *sushi* molds and wooden bowl to be used for preparing the *shari*.

CONDIMENTS AND GARNISHES FOR SUSHI (*ashirai*)

Shiso (perilla frutescens var. crispa)
Commonly known as the beefsteak plant of the mint family. Both reddish-purple and green varieties are available. Easily grown in your herb garden. The young leaves as well as the flower spikes are used. Has a unique fragrance. Edible as is or used for pickling. Seeds available from Asian food stores or mail order from Kitazawa Seed Co., 356 W. Taylor St., San Jose, Ca 95110, U.S.A. or Tsang and Ma Inc., 1306 Old Country Road, Belmont, CA 94002, U.S.A.

Bamboo or nandina leaves
Make attractive non-edible garnishes.

Fresh aspidistra leaves (cast iron plant)
Can be used as a non-edible decoration cut into varied shapes. As an alternative plastic green decorative shapes are sold specifically to place on servings of *sushi*. The striking dark green sets off the white of the rice.

Kinomé (*sansho*—zanthoxylum piperitum—commonly called prickly ash)
Young leaves are used frequently as decorative touches. The leaves are very fragrant and enhance the flavor of Japanese dishes. It is used in soups, pickles, etc. The *sansho* fruit berries are used also and add a pleasant crunch as well as an interesting taste. The *sansho* grows into a tall thick shrub if allowed to reach maturity. This plant is found in certain specialty nurseries in Western United States.

Vegetable garnishes
These are are often utilized. An interesting adaptation is to use a flowering blossom of a cucumber with a miniature cucumber just developing at the tip. Vinegared lotus root is another attractive garnish.

Wasabi (Japanese horseradish—amoracia rusticana)
In the fresh raw state *wasabi* is very expensive in Japan but the flavor is unexcelled. It is an entirely different species from the horseradish found in the United States. Therefore use the powdered canned type. Add a small amount of water to powdered *wasabi* to form a thick paste. Place a plastic wrap or foil cover over the container. Invert the container for 5 minutes so that the intense pungent flavor will develop. It adds much zip and tang to *sushi* as well as your sinuses!

Fresh ginger shoots
These are not readily available in the Western markets so use the packaged imported varieties.

An excellent reference book: "Handbook on Japanese Herbs and Their Uses" is put out by Brooklyn Botanic Garden, 1000 Washington Ave., Brooklyn, N.Y. 11225, U.S.A.

AMAZU SHOGA (Sweet Pickled Ginger)

I suggest in America that since the quality of fresh ginger root is not consistently good, that is, young and of the desirable variety, you purchase the commercially pickled product imported from Japan. It is a natural soft pinkish color achieved by the reaction of the ginger in the rice vinegar marinade. But if you wish to try here is a recipe for you.

Ingredients:
Fresh young ginger root (a large cluster of knobs)
2 teaspoons salt
Marinade:
    2½ tablespoons sugar
    5 tablespoons water
    ¾ cup rice vinegar (*su*)
    dash salt

Method:
Peel ginger. Cut in thin, thin transparent slices. Sprinkle with 2 teaspoons salt. Set aside for one day. Rinse in water to remove excess salt. Cook ginger in boiling water for 5 minutes. Drain. Prepare the vinegar marinade by heating together. Add the cooked ginger while still hot to the marinade solution. Set aside and the color will turn a pale pinkish orange as it cools. This will keep in a covered jar in the refrigerator for weeks.
Amazu shoga is a "go with" for *sushi* . . . such as we associate mustard with hot dogs.

BASIC SEASONED *SUSHI* RICE (*SHARI*)

The flavor of *sushi* rice changes with the seasons. In summer more rice vinegar is used but feel free to make your own flavor adjustments—more sweet or more sour. The basic seasoned vinegar solution (*awase zu*) ratio varies according to the *sushi* type which you prepare. Why? *Sushi* such as *maki-zushi/norimaki* have flavored fillings while *sushi* such as *nigiri-zushi* have no seasonings in the topping (fresh slice of fish) therefore the rice flavor must be suited otherwise there will be conflict of tastes. Even in Japan there are regional likes and dislikes such as we find in our Western sandwich fillings, spaghetti or salad making. Very Important: Rice must be short or medium grain only.

No. 1   Basically for use with *maki-zushi/norimaki*:

Raw rice (short grain or medium only, i.e. Koku-ho, Calrose)	2 cups	3 cups	4 cups
Water	2 cups+2 Tbsp.	3 cups+3 Tbsp.	4 cups+4 Tbsp.
Rice vinegar (*su*)	¼ cup (4 Tbsp.)	6 Tbsp.	½ cup (8 Tbsp.)
Sugar	2 Tbsp.+1½ tsp.	3 Tbsp.+2¼ tsp.	5 Tbsp.
Salt	½ tsp.	¾ tsp.	1 tsp.

No. 2   Basically for use with *saba-zushi*/seasoned fish type *sushi* (salmon or flounder)/for bite-sized *sushi*:

Raw rice (short grain or medium only, i.e. Koku-ho, Calrose)	2 cups	3 cups	4 cups
Water	2 cups+2 Tbsp.	3 cups+3 Tbsp.	4 cups+4 Tbsp.
Rice vinegar (*su*)	¼ cup (4 Tbsp.)	6 Tbsp.	½ cup (8 Tbsp.)
Sugar	1½ tsp.	2¼ tsp.	1 Tbsp.
Salt	1½ tsp.	2¼ tsp.	1 Tbsp.

No. 3   Basically for use with *sushi* with plain ingredients such as *nigiri-zushi/sushi* with conger eel and cucumber:

Raw rice (short grain or medium only, i.e. Koku-ho, Calrose)	2 cups	3 cups	4 cups
Water	2 cups+2 Tbsp.	3 cups+3 Tbsp.	4 cups+4 Tbsp.
Rice vinegar (*su*)	¼ cup (4 Tbsp.)	6 Tbsp.	½ cup (8 Tbsp.)
Sugar	2 Tbsp.	3 Tbsp.	4 Tbsp.
Salt	1 tsp.	1½ tsp.	2 tsp.

Preparation: The *sushi* should be prepared with freshly cooked rice. DO NOT USE long grain rice. It is entirely unsuitable for *sushi*. Cooked rice for *sushi* should be a bit more firm and each grain separate with a slight chewy consistency while still adhering together.

Method:

Wash rice until water is clear. Transfer to a colander. Set aside and drain for 1 hour. Measure the water and add to rice in a heavy pot or electric rice cooker. Bring to a boil, lower heat and allow rice to continue steaming for 15 minutes more with the cover on at all times. Remove from heat. Remove lid. Spread a clean cloth over the pot and recover. Allow to finish steaming without heat for 15 minutes. In the meanwhile mix the rice vinegar, sugar and salt together in a non-aluminum saucepan. Heat and stir to dissolve sugar. Put aside to cool. (Some people just mix these ingredients together, stir to dissolve and do not heat). When the rice is properly steamed take a wooden spatula (*shamoji*) making cutting and turning motions with the rice. Do not smash the kernels.

Get a wooden flat bowl or large platter ready by rubbing the insides with a dampened cloth (vinegar/water solution—*tezu* page 14). Add seasoned rice vinegar solution quickly to the hot rice. Keep fanning the hot rice mixture to remove as much moisture as possible and to cool more quickly. This will achieve a beautiful luster to the rice grains and the result will not be sticky or gummy. This takes about 10 minutes.

Try to keep rice at room temperature. Keep container covered with a clean cloth until you are ready to use the *shari*. It is not to be placed in the refrigerator and should be used within an hour after preparation if possible.

Optional:

Dried kelp (*kombu*), a 4-inch (10 cm) square, for flavor is optional but adds a delicate Japanese flavor to the rice (wipe with a damp cloth prior to use). Place in pot of washed rice with the water and as soon as it comes to boiling point remove the kelp.

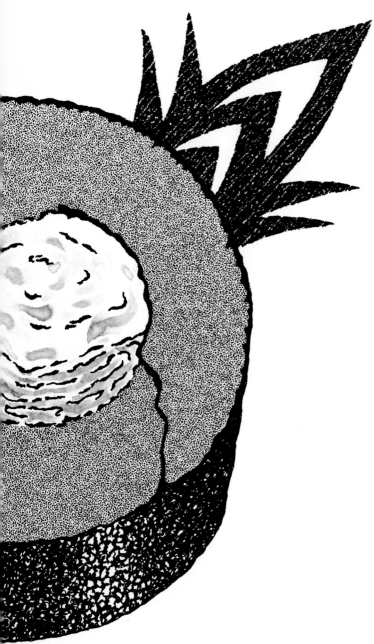

MAKI-ZUSHI

▶
Top: *Chirashi-Zushi*
Bottom: *Maki-Zushi (Norimaki/Futomaki)*

HOW TO MAKE INGREDIENTS

■ THIN EGGSHEETS (*Usuyaki Tamago*)

Similar to a crêpe. Used for garnishes, *maki-zushi/norimaki*, stuffed and folded *sushi*.

Ingredients:
8 eggs
2 tablespoons sugar
pinch salt
½ teaspoon cornstarch dissolved in 1 tablespoon water
oil for greasing pan

Method:
Mix well with chopsticks. Strain through a sieve or a cheesecloth. Heat an 8-inch (20 cm) square pan. Oil pan. Wipe off any excess with paper towels. Pour in 1½ tablespoons of egg mixture. Shake pan to even the egg in pan. Cook over low heat. When surface begins to dry, use chopsticks to loosen edges. Then insert halfway to flip the eggsheet over. Cook for another minute to firm up. Transfer to a cookie rack and cool. Repeat process until all egg mixture is used. Yields 8 eggsheets. Cornstarch in this recipe helps to keep eggsheet firm.

THIN EGGSHEETS

KAMPYO

22

■ ROLLED OMELET (*Atsuyaki Tamago*) Recipe #1

Ingredients:

5 eggs
3 tablespoons sugar

dash salt
oil for greasing pan

Method:

Beat eggs. Mix with sugar and salt. Strain through cheesecloth or sieve. Heat an 8-inch (20 cm) square pan. Oil pan. Remove excess with a paper towel. Pour in ⅓ of egg mixture to cover entire pan. When half cooked and a bit firm, roll mixture in front of you jelly-roll style away from you and slide it all back toward yourself. Oil the emptied space. Add more egg mixture and roll away from you again when half cooked. Oil again. Add remaining egg mixture. Cook and roll for the final time. Each time original roll is the core. Allow this large egg roll to set a minute prior to transferring to a cutting board. Cool and slice in ¾-inch (19 mm) widths.

Variation: This can be fried as a thick ¼-inch (6 mm) omelet-style to be cut in ¼-inch (6 mm) square strips for *maki-zushi* filling.

■ ROLLED OMELET (*Atsuyaki Tamago*) Recipe #2

Ingredients:

6 eggs
1 tablespoon sugar or more
6 tablespoons *dashi*, soup stock or water
½ teaspoon salt
1 teaspoon *mirin* or sherry

Method:

Mix all ingredients together. Heat square frying pan and oil very lightly. Pour ¼ cupful of the egg mixture into the hot pan and cook over low heat until the egg is firm but not dry. Starting closest to the handle of the frying pan, roll the egg away like a jelly-roll and slide it back all toward yourself. Oil pan lightly again and pour another ¼ cupful of mixture into pan. When it is set, roll the first roll onto the new sheet and continue this process until all of the egg is used. Each layer of egg should be partially cooked rather soft in the center. Not dry. Turn onto a board and cut into 1-inch (2.5 cm) thick slices. Will serve 6. This is a nice addition to a picnic lunch. A few par-boiled peas could be sprinkled onto the cooking eggsheets for a variation in color—just a sprinkle.

■ *KAMPYO* (Dried Gourd Shavings)

Ingredients:

2 oz.(50 g) dried gourd shavings
1 cup *dashi*
5 tablespoons sugar
5 tablespoons *mirin* (Japanese sweet rice wine)
4 tablespoons *shoyu*

Method:

Wash dried gourd shavings (*kampyo*) in water. Rub with salt until soft. Rinse salt off in water. Soak in water for an hour. Bring to a boil and drain off water. Add *dashi*. Cook until crisp-tender. Add sugar, *mirin* and *shoyu*. Cook over medium heat until juices have evaporated. Cool on a plate.

ANAGO

OBORO

EBI

SHIITAKE

■ ANAGO (Seasoned Conger Eel)

Ingredients:
2 conger eels
½ cup *mirin* (Japanese sweet rice wine)
¼ cup *shoyu*
1 teaspoon sugar

Method:
Skin eels to remove slime. Cut vertically in half from the back side. Align side by side. Spear with skewers. Broil over high heat. Turn over and broil other side. Put *mirin, shoyu* and sugar in pan. Bring to a boil. Add broiled conger eel. Take conger eel from pan. Boil down juice. Place conger eel in pan to absorb extra juices. Substitute: Use canned *unagi kabayaki*.

■ OBORO (Mashed Cod Fish or Shrimp)

Ingredients:
2–4 pieces 15 oz.(400 g) cod fish or shrimp
2 or 3 tablespoons sugar
dash salt
1 tablespoon *saké* (Japanese rice wine)
dash red food coloring

Method:
Place cod fish and enough water to cover in pan. Cook for 6–7 minutes. Do not worry about the white foam bubbles. Put pan in sink. Rinse under running water. When water becomes clear, turn off. Remove skin and bones. Put fish in strainer. Drain. Wrap fish in a cloth. Squeeze out excess water. Grind in a mortar. Put in a frying pan. Add seasonings and red coloring. Cook over low heat. Mix well with chopsticks. Turn away from heat occasionally and then return back to the stove. Mix well until fluffy. For shrimp cook only 3–4 minutes. Rinse, peel and mash. Proceed to cook in same manner as the fish *oboro*.

■ EBI (Cooked Shrimp)

Remove veins with skewer. Spear with skewer from the tail through the head portion to prevent curling. Add shrimp to boiling water with salt. Cook for 3–4 minutes. When shrimp is done remove skewers. Shell. Butterfly-cut if required for recipe.

■ SEASONED SHIITAKE

Ingredients:
10 dried *shiitake* (black Japanese forest mushrooms)
1½ cups lukewarm water
5 tablespoons sugar
5 tablespoons *mirin* (Japanese sweet rice wine)
4 tablespoons *shoyu*

Method:
Wash *shiitake*. Soak in lukewarm water until soft for 20 minutes. If a dash of sugar is added they will soften quicker. Remove mushrooms from soaking liquid. Pour this liquid into a small saucepan being sure that you do not use the sediment at the bottom. Add mushrooms and seasonings. Cover and simmer until liquid has evaporated.

NORIMAKI

CHUMAKI or FUTOMAKI
(Rolled *maki-zushi/norimaki* in a standard size roll)

Ingredients:
2 cups vinegared rice (*shari*) #1, see page 18
6 dried *shiitake* (black Japanese forest mushrooms)
1 oz. (30 g) *kampyo*
3 eggs
10 *mitsuba* (trefoil) or substitute watercress, cooked fresh string beans or
   cooked spinach (cook only briefly to keep good green color)
8 tablespoons tangle flakes (*oboro kombu*)
2 sheets *nori*, toasted one side
shoyu (soy sauce)
salt
sugar
oil

Method:
Prepare vinegared rice (*shari*). Put aside.

Soak dried *shiitake* in ½ cup warm water. Cut and discard stems. Slice in thin strips. Cook in the soaking liquid (do not use the sediment at the bottom however). Add 4 tablespoons *shoyu* and 3 tablespoons sugar. Cook *kampyo* after rubbing well with salt. Rinse in water. Fill a pan with *kampyo* and 2–3 tablespoons water, 5 tablespoons sugar and 3 tablespoons *shoyu*. Cook until liquid is absorbed.

Beat eggs. Mix with 1 tablespoon sugar and dash salt. Heat a frying pan. Oil pan and remove excess. Pour egg mixture to make an eggsheet. Cut according to the length of the *nori*.

Dip *mitsuba* in boiling water to blanch slightly. Lay out a dry cloth on the *sudaré*. Place the toasted *nori* thereon. Spread out some vinegared rice. Leave a ½-inch (12 mm) strip of *nori* exposed at the end furthest from your body. Place the tangle flakes (*oboro kombu*), egg strip, *shiitake*, *kampyo* and *mitsuba* in the center. Dampen exposed strip of *nori* with vinegar/water solution. Roll up with *sudaré* from the front going away from you. Press the ends to shape. Place the *chumaki* with the seam on the bottom. Cut rolled *chumaki* in 6 or 8 pieces. In between cuts clean your knife so you can slice skillfully.

Variations: Use fresh mushrooms which have been seasoned, sweet cooked carrots or bamboo shoots. For Western adaptations use ham, roast pork, chicken, cheese, scrambled egg, cucumber slices or shrimp.

ASSORTED *NORIMAKI*

HOSOMAKI

A slender version of *maki-zushi/norimaki*. The filling is usually of one ingredient instead of the assortment found in the larger *maki-zushi/norimaki*.

Ingredients:
2 cups vinegared rice (*shari*) #1, see page 18
1 oz.(30 g) *kampyo* (dried gourd shavings)
5 sheets *nori* (laver seaweed)
salt
rice vinegar (*su*)
sugar
shoyu

Method:
Prepare vinegared rice (*shari*). Put aside.

Cut the *kampyo* strips in 3 pieces. Rub with salt. Rinse in water. Cook in enough boiling water until soft. Drain. Squeeze out the water. Fill a pan with the *kampyo* and add 2–3 tablespoons water, 5 tablespoons sugar and 3 tablespoons *shoyu*. Cook until the liquid is absorbed.

Toast 2 *nori* sheets together over low heat. Turn off the heat when the color of the *nori* becomes greenish. Do not overtoast. Cut in half crosswise—the piece will measure approximately 7 by 4 inches (17.5 × 10 cm).

Place *nori* on the surface of *sudaré*. So the longest length will be crosswise. Moisten hands with *tezu* (vinegar/water) solution, see page 14. Make a ball of ½ cup prepared vinegared rice (*shari*). Place this mound on the *nori*. Spread out carefully leaving about ½ inch (12 mm) of the *nori* exposed on the end furthest away from you.

Make a hollow groove in the center so you can place 3 pieces of cooked *kampyo* lengthwise. Dampen exposed strip of *nori* with vinegar/water solution. Lift the front of the *sudaré* closest to your body. Roll the *hosomaki* with the *sudaré* pressing down on the *nori* portion firmly and finally it will stick to itself when completely rolled. Shape the roll ends so no rice will fall out. If you can let it rest a minute or two all the better. Moisten a sharp knife with vinegared water. Ideal manner of cutting is in half and then wiping the knife and placing the two rolls together. Cut the two rolls together again in half to result in 4 pieces.

Variations for filling:
TEKKA MAKI (rolled *hosomaki* with tuna)
Use a strip of fresh tuna cut ½-inch (12 mm) square lengthwise. Serve with *wasabi*.
KAPPA MAKI (rolled *hosomaki* with cucumber)
Rub cucumber with salt. Rinse with water. Cut cucumber into spears lengthwise. Sprinkle toasted white sesame seeds to give good flavor.
SHINKO MAKI (rolled *hosomaki* with pickled radish)
Use pickled radish (*takuan*) or other pickled vegetable as the filling. Slice pickles lengthwise. The taste is sweet/sour/tangy and delicious. A nice variation with the other *sushi*. See page 30 for other *hosomaki* filling ideas. Devise your own!

MORE *HOSOMAKI/NORIMAKI*

Cross sliced sections: Each *hosomaki/norimaki* uses one-half sheet of toasted *nori* cut lengthwise with a layer of vinegared rice (*shari*) plus a center core filling.

These are like sandwich filling ideas. Use whatever is your fancy. This method utilizes the same process as assorted *hosomaki* page 27.

1. Pickled yellow radish (*takuan*) is used for the core. Slice pickled radish in strips. Mix *takuan* with toasted white sesame seeds and *mirin* (Japanese sweet rice wine). Spread pickles lengthwise on the vinegared rice (*shari*) and roll up firmly.

2. *Gobo* (burdock) pickled with *miso* (bean paste) is used for the core. Remove *miso* from the burdock. Dip in *mirin* (Japanese sweet rice wine). Slice *gobo* lengthwise in ¼-inch (6 mm) strips. Place in center of rice roll.

3. Omelet is used for the core. Add 1 tablespoon sugar, dash salt and 2 teaspoons *mirin* to 2 beaten eggs. Mix well. Fry an omelet. Cool, slice lengthwise. Place in center of *hosomaki*.

4. Cooked *shiitake* is used for core. Soak 4 dried *shiitake* in water about 15–20 minutes. Cut off stem portion. Cook in soaking water, being careful not to use sediment at the bottom of the water. Add 1 tablespoon *shoyu*, 1 tablespoon sugar and 1 tablespoon *mirin* mixed together. Cook until juice has evaporated. Slice in ½-inch (12 mm) lengths. Place in center of *norimaki*.

5. Sprinkle a little *saké* (Japanese rice wine) on red salmon roe (*ikura*). Separate the eggs. Place roe in center of the rice mixture. Roll up, being careful not to crush the eggs.

6. *Mitsuba* (trefoil) and vegetables pickled with horseradish are used for this core. Cook *mitsuba* in boiling water until just wilted. Dip in some salted water. Drain. Use for core of *hosomaki*.

7. Cheese and *katsuobushi* (bonito flakes) are basis for this filling. Cut cheese julienne strips. Dip bonito flakes in some *shoyu*. Place in center for core of *norimaki*.

8. Sliced *shiso* (beefsteak plant) and chopped salt-pickled plum (*umeboshi*) are used for the core. Cut beefsteak plant leaves lengthwise in half. Remove seed from *umeboshi*. Chop. Add drops of *mirin*. Roll up the *hosomaki*.

9. *Wasabi* is used for this core. Soak 1 ounce dried gourd shavings (*kampyo*) in water. Rub with salt until soft. Cook in ¼ cup boiling water, adding 2 teaspoons *dashi*, 1 tablespoon *shoyu*, 1 teaspoon sugar and 1 tablespoon *mirin*. Allow juices to evaporate. Place in center of *norimaki*.

10. Add *mirin* to sea urchin roe (*uni*). Mix well. Spread sea urchin mixture on the vinegared rice center. Roll up.
    Dream up your own variation!

1

4

8

2

5

9

3

6

10

7

HANA-ZUSHI

Sushi made to appear like flowers in a simple yet very artistic design. The Japanese are known for their aesthetic way with foods. This is a perfect example of Japanese food art prepared with extreme care and much love for the diner's enjoyment.

Prepare vinegared rice (*shari*) #1, see page 18. If you desire to make many of these I would suggest you prepare 2 cups of raw rice to begin with and then as you become more experienced you can cook more rice quantity.

CHRYSANTHEMUM *SUSHI*

Ingredients:
⅔ cup cooked prepared vinegared rice (*shari*)
a half sheet of *nori*, toasted (whole sheet should be cut lengthwise in half)
1 tablespoon mashed fish seasoned with dashes of sugar and *mirin* and a few drops
    red food coloring or substitute shrimp *oboro*, see page 25
2–3 fresh string beans
eggsheet (thin omelet, see page 41), thinly shredded

Method:
Make mashed fish and season. Cook fresh string beans in boiling water with salt for about 3–4 minutes. Slice in long thin strips. Place *nori* on *sudaré*. Leave ½ inch (12 mm) on both edges of *nori* without any rice. See sketch. Place vinegared rice on the toasted *nori*. Place mashed fish and beans in a center line on the rice. Add a dab of vinegar/water solution on the edges of the *nori* so that you can stick the two edges when they come together. Wrap up with the *sudaré*. Shape the roll into flower petals. Cut one rolled bar into 7 portions and arrange to simulate a chrysanthemum flower. Top with sliced egg shreds in center. Chrysanthemum leaves are shown in the picture along with the "flower *sushi*." A garnish of *beni shoga*, shredded, is placed to balance the visual "picture" as well as to be eaten with the *sushi*.

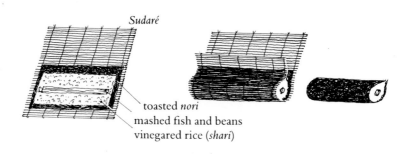

Sudaré

toasted *nori*
mashed fish and beans
vinegared rice (*shari*)

WISTERIA *SUSHI*

Ingredients:

⅔ cup cooked prepared vinegared rice (*shari*)

a half sheet of *nori*, toasted (whole sheet should be cut lengthwise in half)

1 teaspoon mashed fish seasoned with dashes of sugar and *mirin* with a few
   drops of red food coloring or substitute shrimp *oboro*, see page 25

1 long piece of watercress or parsley stem

Method:

Place the toasted *nori* on *sudaré*. Place the vinegared rice on the *nori* leaving the two edges of the *nori* exposed without rice. Dampen the edges of the *nori* as per sketch. Stick both ends of the *nori* together. Wrap up with *sudaré*. Cut into 9 pieces. Shape with fingers to make the slices appear as petals of the wisteria as per picture. Dab a bit of *oboro* in the center of each slice and arrange the slices to make it appear like a spray of wisteria flowers. Use the watercress or parsley stem as the flower vein.

FOR ROLLING *SUSHI* (*MAKI-ZUSHI/NORIMAKI*)

Rolling sushi appears simple enough until one actually begins the process and sometimes the filling is off center, the *nori* doesn't match the other side when completely rolled, the *maki-zushi/norimaki* is very loosely grained with rice instead of the firmness which is ideal and even the sliced *maki-zushi* practically falls apart as you bring it to your mouth to eat with your fingers! But do not despair. All this takes experience and unless one tries one cannot know or experience the "method." The main precaution when you roll with *sudaré* is to firmly press on the roll to compress the rice kernels. And to begin with your rice must not be overly soft or too hard. There must be a certain chewy texture much as spaghetti is cooked al dente.

1. Toast 2 *nori* sheets held together diagonally. See picture. Toast over low heat on one side of each *nori* sheet leaving the inside portion untoasted. A good aroma, a distictive flavor and a crispness will be your result. Do not overtoast. High heat causes the *nori* to dampen.

2. Place a *sudaré* (bamboo rolling mat) on a dry chopping board. Spread toasted *nori* on the *sudaré* leaving a ⅜-inch (9 mm) space or/more at the farthest point away from you when placing the vinegared rice (*shari*) thereon prior to rolling.

Approximately a heaping rice bowl of cooked vinegar seasoned rice is necessary for one roll. About 4½ cups cooked rice is necessary for 4 rolls. Rice may be as warm as your body temperature when using for *maki-zushi/norimaki*. If it is too cold it will not stick together very well.

Caution: Be sure that the filling is the same temperature as the rice. If not—such as ice cold filling plus warm rice the chance for spoilage is very great. If one has made up the filling the day before reheat it again and bring to room temperature for safety.

3. Spread vinegared rice on *nori* in an even layer. Do not crush the rice grains. Before rice sticks to your fingers moisten in vinegar/water (*tezu*), see page 14. Dab vinegar/water mixture on the exposed *nori* sheet edge. This will help to stick the *nori* edge as you roll the *maki-zushi*.
4. Be sure ingredients have excess moisture or juices wiped off. Make a groove along the center of the rice mixture on the *sudaré*. Fill the groove with the prepared ingredients. Use the *sudaré* mat to roll *sushi* jelly-roll style. This helps make a firm *maki-zushi*.
5. Firm both ends of the rice mixture by pressing down after rolling and the *maki-zushi* is still surrounded by the mat. Remove *sudaré* and place seam side down on platter until ready to cut.
6. Moisten knife with a damp vinegared cloth. Slice by cutting the roll in half and then slicing each half into 4 equal portions. Clean the knife between cuts to prevent sticking and messy cutting.

Extra tip: I have tested leftover *maki-zushi* by wrapping well in aluminum foil and putting in the freezer for a few days. I brought back to room temperature an hour prior to use. Removed the foil and rewrapped in plastic wrap. Placed the completely wrapped roll in the microwave and heated it less than a minute. It was most acceptable and better than having to toss it out. Not exactly as fresh as "just made" but still good. Normally *sushi* is not refrigerated since the rice gets hard. But if you do have some leftover do not be afraid to cover it well with foil and place in the refrigerator. Serve room temperature however. It will spoil readily so be cautious.

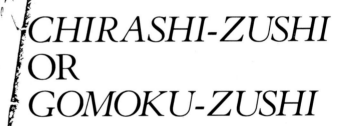

CHIRASHI-ZUSHI OR GOMOKU-ZUSHI

Edo (Tokyo) Chirashi-zushi style places the seasoned ingredients scattered on top of the vinegared rice (*shari*) in a bowl.

Kansai (Kyoto, Osaka) Chirashi-zushi style mixes the seasoned ingredients with the vinegared rice (*shari*) and after putting the mixture in a bowl eggsheet strips garnish the top surface.

GOMOKU-ZUSHI

This is a very tempting "meal in one" *sushi*. Preparation may be tedious but once learned it is not difficult. You will begin to take all kinds of short-cuts as you become more familiar.

Ingredients:
3 cups vinegared rice (*shari*) #1, see page 18
2 eggs
1 oz.(30 g) edible pod peas (Chinese snow peas)
1 chunk lotus root (see ingredients for *gomoku-zushi* for using dried lotus root
   if fresh not available)
1 carrot
⅔ oz.(20 g) dried *kampyo* (gourd shavings)
4 dried *shiitake* (black Japanese forest mushrooms)
3 *agé* (fried soybean cakes)
2 sheets *nori* (laver seaweed)

Method:
Prepare vinegared rice (*shari*). Put aside.
For topping (Ingredients A)
Use carrot cut in floral shapes, vinegared lotus root, *kinshi tamago* (sliced eggsheet), cooked edible pod peas or substitute green peas.
Refer to page 42 for cooking/seasoning ingredients.
For mixing together (Ingredients B)
Use sweet carrot pieces left over from making carrot flowers, seasoned cooked *kampyo*, seasoned *shiitake*, sweet cooked *agé*, vinegared lotus root pieces left over from making shapes for topping (if desired can be included in rice mixture). Cut prepared ingredients into ¼-½-inch (6-13 mm) pieces.
For garnishing (Ingredients C)
Toasted sesame seeds and toasted *nori* (laver seaweed) cut into thin strips.

Final preparation:
Combine cooled vinegared rice with the prepared Ingredients B. Mix well. Place lightly in shallow bowls. Garnish with ingredients A and C in an aesthetic design of colors and textures.

How to prepare:
Ingredients for *Chirashi-Zushi*
Gomoku-zushi and *chirashi-zushi* are basically one and the same *sushi*. Regional styles make for different names. As well as the placement of the ingredients whether mixed with the vinegared rice (*shari*) or placed separately on top as a garnish for the vinegared rice (*shari*). Choose whichever name you like better. *Chirashi* literally means to scatter.

■ *TAMAGO YAKI* (Rolled Sweet Omelet)

This omelet can be used also as a side dish to be served with *sushi*.

Ingredients:

4 eggs	dash salt
2 tablespoons sugar	1 tablespoon water or *dashi*

Method:

Beat eggs in bowl. Mix well with sugar and salt. By adding water or *dashi* to the egg mixture the omelet will be fluffier. Heat a square frying pan over medium heat. Oil pan lightly. Pour in ⅓ of the egg mixture to cover the entire pan. Cook over medium heat. Before the surface begins to dry, roll egg mixture to the front toward you jelly-roll style. Move the rolled egg away from you to the far end of pan. Oil the emptied space. Grasp the handle of the pan and tilt. Add ⅓ of the egg mixture under the rolled egg. Continue to fry. Make a continuing jelly-roll omelet again and push away from you. Oil the back half of the pan again. Add the balance of the egg mixture. Roll toward you again. This will result in one big fat jelly-roll type omelet. Transfer this rolled omelet to a cutting board. Cut in ½–¾-inch (12–19 mm) slices. A small piece of cheesecloth is useful for oiling the pan.

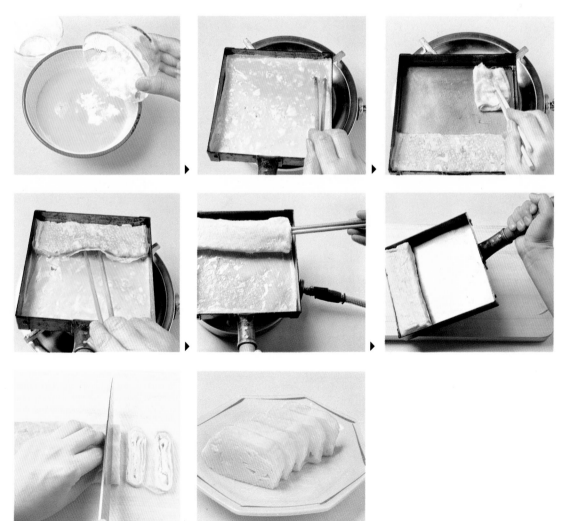

■ KINSHI TAMAGO (Egg Strips)

This can be used for garnishing as well as for an ingredient in *Chirashi-zushi/Gomoku-zushi*.

Ingredients:
2 eggs
dash salt
2 teaspoons sugar

Method:
Beat eggs in a bowl and mix well with salt and sugar. Strain. Heat a round frying pan over medium heat. Oil pan lightly. Remove any excess oil. Pour in ⅓ of the egg mixture to cover entire pan. Shake frying pan to spread the egg evenly over surface. Fry over low heat.

When surface begins to dry use chopsticks to loosen the edges. Then insert halfway to flip the egg omelet over. Remove to slicing board. Fold in three. Cut in strips. Depending upon usage: cut thick or thin widths.

■ SWEET CARROTS

1 carrot
½ teaspoon sugar
dash salt

Slice carrot in ½-inch (12 mm) rings and cut in floral shapes. (There are special metal cutters in miniature size that can be used.) Place carrots in pan with water barely covering. Add sugar and salt. Cook until tender about 4 minutes. Cut remaining carrot pieces into strips. Cook in the same boiling water.

■ SEASONED *SHIITAKE* MUSHROOMS

4 dried *shiitake* (black Japanese forest mushrooms)
1½ tablespoons sugar

1½ tablespoons *shoyu*
½ tablespoon *mirin* (sweet rice wine)

Soak dried *shiitake* in warm water 20 minutes until soft. Remove stems and discard. Cut into thin strips.

Cook in soaking liquid making sure that you discard the portion at the bottom which has sediment. Add sugar, *shoyu* and *mirin*. Cook until juices have been absorbed.

■ COOKED EDIBLE POD PEAS

1 oz.(30 g) edible pod peas (snow peas, China peas, sweet pea pods, etc.)

String edible pod peas. Cook peas in boiling water 1 minute. Drain. Green beans can be substituted in which case cook a few extra minutes. Basically the substitution is for the green color. Even frozen peas could be used.

■ VINEGARED LOTUS ROOT

Lotus root is an interesting vegetable. Very decorative in appearance with its many holes. Since it is seasonal and not always available, one can substitute already seasoned vinegared lotus root sold in small packets for *sushi* recipes. Dried lotus root is available. This can be reconstituted with water and vinegared in similar manner as follows.

Ingredients:
¼ lb.(120 g) fresh lotus root   3 tablespoons sugar
½ teaspoon salt   2 tablespoons rice vinegar (*su*)

Method:
Peel lotus root. Cut root in 2-inch (5 cm) thick chunks. Soak in cold water mixed with 2 tablespoons rice vinegar. Cut edges between the holes in V-shaped darts and remove little pieces. This will form flower shaped lotus slices. Slice thinly. Cook lotus root over high heat in ½ cup boiling water with salt and sugar added. Do not cover. Marinate in extra rice vinegar for good flavor.

If using dried lotus root slices place in cold water to cover overnight. Slices will expand greatly. Proceed to use as fresh. Lotus root can be used in any recipe in similar fashion as carrots are used. An interesting crunchy texture. Try deep-frying. Delicious—similar to French fries!

ADDITIONAL INGREDIENTS WHICH
COULD BE USED:

■ COOKED SHRIMP

8 raw shrimp, heads removed
1 tablespoon *saké* (Japanese rice wine)
1 teaspoon salt
dash rice vinegar (*su*)

Remove black veins. Keep tail intact. Spear shrimp with skewers or toothpicks from tail to head to prevent curling. Fill pot with cold water barely to cover bottom. Bring to a boil. Place shrimp, *saké* and salt in water. Cook for 3–4 minutes.

Shell shrimp but leave tails intact. Split carefully from the inner section so that the sharp knife will not cut all the way through at the back (butterfly method). Before using sprinkle rice vinegar over shrimp.

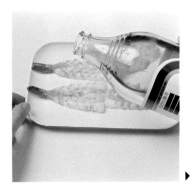 

■ VINEGARED MACKEREL Refer to *Shimesaba* page 84

■ *SANSHO*

Fresh *sansho* leaves may be used if available. Soak in water to make crisp. Before serving, pat dry with paper towels. *Sansho* may be used in soup also.

■ VINEGARED GIZZARD SHAD

3 gizzard shad or Spanish mackerel (*aji*), small size
dash salt
rice vinegar (*su*)

Split gizzard shad or mackerel carefully at the back with a sharp knife but do not cut all the way through. Sprinkle with salt. Set aside for 15 minutes. Rinse salt off with vinegar. Place in plate. (Pyrex pie plate would be ideal). Soak in vinegar for ten minutes. Discard vinegar. Cut into bite-size pieces.

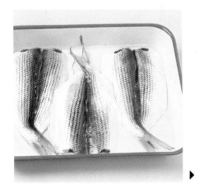

■ SEASONED BAMBOO SHOOTS (*Takenoko*)

2 small bamboo shoots (boiled)
⅓ cup water or *dashi*
2 teaspoons *shoyu*
1 teaspoon *mirin* (Japanese sweet rice wine)

Cut in slices less than ¼ inch (6 mm) thick. Wash any white sediment which may still be on the shoot. Put water or *dashi* in small pan. Cook bamboo shoots with *shoyu* and *mirin* over medium heat until juices are absorbed.

■ SEASONED DRIED GOURD SHAVINGS (*Kampyo*)

⅔ oz.(20 g) dried gourd shavings (*kampyo*)
2½ tablespoons *shoyu*
3 tablespoons sugar
1 tablespoon *mirin* (Japanese sweet rice wine)

Wash dried *kampyo*. Rub with salt until soft. Rinse salt off in water. Soak in water for 30–40 minutes until soft if time is available. Cook in boiling water for 7–8 minutes. Drain water. Add seasonings and cook over low heat until the juices are absorbed. Do not scorch. Cool.

■ TOASTED SESAME SEEDS (*Iri Goma*)

Heat frying pan. Use no oil. Toast sesame seeds in pan over low heat stirring with a large wooden spoon. Continue to heat until seeds jump. Do not burn! Transfer seeds to paper or cloth. Mince the seeds so more flavor will be released. If any recipe calls for ground or pulverized sesame seeds then use a *suribachi* to make a paste. The flavor is excitingly aromatic! Wonderful!

■ SWEET FRIED *AGÉ* (Fried Soybean Cakes)

3 *agé* (fried soybean cakes)
¾ cup *dashi* or water
3 tablespoons sugar
2½ tablespoons *shoyu*
1 teaspoon *mirin* (Japanese sweet rice wine)

Pour boiling water over the *agé* in order to remove some of the excess oil. If you feel the *agé* is still too greasy soak in boiling water and again drain off the excess. Cut vertically in half. Then cut crosswise into thin strips. Cook in boiling water or *dashi* with balance of ingredients over medium heat until liquid has evaporated.

■ CRUMBLED TOASTED *NORI* (Laver Seaweed)

Hold one edge of the *nori* sheet. Toast over low heat quickly on one side to make crisp. Do not burn. When the color turns green and a good aroma is given off turn off heat. Takes only seconds. Wrap in a dry cloth and crumble. Or do so between palms of your hands over a plate.

GOMOKU-ZUSHI

Ingredients:

3 cups raw rice (short or medium grain), i.e.
Kokuho or Calrose

3⅓ cups water

1 piece *kombu* (kelp seaweed) 5 inches (10
cm) square

Vinegar seasoning:
4½ tablespoons rice vinegar (*su*)
3 tablespoons sugar
1 tablespoon salt

Sushi Ingredients:
1 medium size carrot

1 or 2 *gobo* (burdock root)

3 strips *kampyo* (dried gourd shavings)

1 piece *renkon* (lotus root), if available

4 medium size dried *shiitake* (black
Japanese forest mushroom)

3 pieces 1½-inch (3.7 cm) square *koyadofu*

Garnish:
1 can *kabayaki unagi* (broiled eel), mashed
2 eggs
2 sheets *nori* (laver seaweed)
beni shoga (red pickled ginger) sliced

Method:

Mix vinegar seasoning together in a non-metallic bowl.

Wash rice well. Drain and allow to stand for 1 hour. Place rice in a rice cooker or heavy pot with a tight lid. Add water and piece of *kombu*. As soon as it comes to boil, remove kelp and put aside for other uses or discard. This kelp is added to give a subtle sweet touch of flavor to the rice. Continue to boil with cover for about 3 minutes. Then reduce heat to medium for another 5 minutes. Allow rice to steam on low heat for 15 minutes or until all moisture has been absorbed. Keep lid on tightly so steam will not escape. Remove from heat. Wait 10 minutes. Lightly transfer rice to a shallow wooden bowl, if available. While tossing rice kernels (do not smash) add the vinegar seasonings. Continue to fan to cool while you still loosely fold the rice kernels with rice paddle.

While the rice mixture is still hot add the ingredients which were prepared while the rice was cooking.

How to prepare *sushi* ingredients:

Shred carrot in 2-inch (5 cm) lengths. Fry in 1 teaspoon oil. Pour 2 tablespoons water over carrot. Parboil 1 minute, add 1 tablespoon sugar and ¼ teaspoon salt. Cook down until liquid evaporates.

Shave *gobo* root in thin diagonal shavings. Fry in hot skillet with 1 teaspoon oil. Add 1½ tablespoons water, 1 tablespoon sugar, 1 teaspoon *shoyu* and ¼ teaspoon salt. Simmer until liquid evaporates.

Slice *renkon* and cook with 1½ tablespoons water, 1 tablespoon sugar, 1 teaspoon *shoyu* and ¼ teaspoon salt. Simmer until liquid evaporates.

Soak dried gourd shavings in water. Rub with salt. Rinse. Add 1½ tablespoons water and 1 tablespoon sugar and cook down. Chop into ¼-inch (6 mm) pieces.

Soak *shiitake* in warm water for 15 minutes. Squeeze out excess water. Boil in 1 tablespoon water, 1 teaspoon sugar and dash salt until liquid evaporates. Slice.

Soak dried *koyadofu* in boiling water. Cover. Allow to stand 3-5 minutes until *koyadofu* gets swollen with water. Pour off water and add cold water. Press between hands to release excess water and all residue. Soak one more time in cold water and repeat pressing process. Cut into 1½ by ¼-inch (4 × 0.6 cm) strips. Add 1½ tablespoons water, 1½ tablespoons sugar, 1 teaspoon *shoyu* and dash salt. Cook until moisture is absorbed

Prepare the garnish: Mash *unagi* (eel). Put aside. Beat 2 eggs and lightly oil hot skillet. Make 2 thin omelets over medium heat. Cut in thin shreds

Toast *nori* sheets lightly on one side for the flavor and the aroma to become intensified. *Nori* can be cut in thin strips or crumbled. Serve the rice mixture in a large deep bowl placing the garnish ingredients on top in a decorative manner with the sliced ginger forming a rose design.

This *sushi* mixture can be served slightly warm or at room temperature.

Bara-Zushi with Mackerel

Bara-Zushi with Crab

KANSAI-STYLE *BARA-ZUSHI*

In *Kansai*-style *bara-zushi* (scattered rice) the vinegared rice plus the flavored ingredients are mixed together. The rice kernels absorb much good flavor and it is a tasty way to prepare *sushi*. You will no doubt come up with your own combinations in very short order. It is actually a light meal in itself and depending upon the ingredients it can be inexpensive or expensive.

BARA-ZUSHI WITH CRAB

Ingredients:
2 cups vinegared rice (*shari*) #1, see page 18
1 *koyadofu* (dehydrated bean curd)
1 canned bamboo shoot or 1 fresh boiled bamboo shoot, if available
½ can crab, shredded and cartilages removed
2 eggs
½ tablespoon toasted white sesame seeds
½ sheet *nori* (laver seaweed)
1 tablespoon green peas (fresh or frozen)
a little sweet pickled ginger (*amazu shoga*), optional
shoyu, salt, rice vinegar, sugar, *mirin* (Japanese sweet rice wine) and oil

Method:
Prepare vinegared rice. Put aside.

Put dried bean curd in a bowl. Pour some boiling water to cover. Set aside until soft. Add a little cold water so you can handle it. Remove and press the bean curd between the palms of your hands and squeeze out the excess water.

Add 2 teaspoons sugar, 1 teaspoon *mirin*, dash salt, 1 teaspoon *shoyu* to 1 cup water. Bring to a boil. Put in the reconstituted bean curd. Boil down until most of the liquid is absorbed. Cool. Cut the flavored bean curd into ¼-inch (6 mm) cubes without squeezing out the juices. Cut bamboo shoots into ¼-inch (6 mm) cubes. Dip in boiling water. Mix ½ cup water, 1 teaspoon sugar, 1 teaspoon *mirin*, dash salt and ½ teaspoon *shoyu*. Cook the bamboo cubes in this mixture until the juices are evaporated. Put aside.

Sprinkle 1 tablespoon rice vinegar and a dash of salt on the shredded crabmeat. Set aside for 15 minutes.

Beat eggs. Add a dash of salt. Heat pan. Lightly oil pan. Pour egg mixture into pan. Cook over medium heat to make a thin eggsheet. Slice in thin strips.

Toast the *nori* briefly to bring out the flavor. Rub between palms of hands to crumble. Put aside. Dip green peas in boiling water for a few seconds to cook slightly. Slice ginger into strips.

Mix prepared vinegared rice (*shari*) with bean curd pieces, bamboo cubes, crabmeat and toasted sesame seeds. Lightly scoop onto plates. Garnish with egg strips, *nori* crumbled pieces, green peas and the ginger strips (optional).

BARA-ZUSHI WITH SHRIMP

This recipe utilizes a blending of familiar ingredients to achieve a simple meal. The egg mixture is sweet since the Japanese like it this way.

Ingredients:
2 cups vinegared rice (*shari*) #1, see page 18
4 eggs
4 tablespoons cooked shrimp, minced and pulverized
2 tablespoons *saké* (Japanese rice wine)
2 tablespoons sugar
1 small cucumber
1 sheet of *nori* (laver seaweed)
Japanese *sansho* plant sprigs (prickly ash—zanthoxylum piperitum), if available,
    for garnish otherwise substitute watercress or parsley
salt, sugar and *saké*

Method:
Prepare vinegared rice (*shari*). Put aside.
    Combine shrimp paste with *saké*. Beat eggs. Add mixed shrimp paste and sugar. Mix well. Fry in oiled hot skillet over medium heat. Scramble mixture using a fork or by holding 5–6 chopsticks together like a many tined fork.
    Slice cucumber into thin rounds. Salt slightly. Let stand 5 minutes. Squeeze out the water which is drawn out of the cucumber by the salt reaction.
    Toast *nori* sheet over a gas or electric burner for a few seconds. Crumble. Set aside.
    Mix prepared vinegared rice with ⅓ of the scrambled egg mixture, cucumber and *nori*.
    Serve on dishes. Top with the remaining ⅔ of the scrambled egg mixture. Garnish with fresh *sansho* or whatever you desire.

BARA-ZUSHI WITH MACKEREL

A unique approach to using marinated fish and vegetables with rice. The pickled *shiso* buds add a crunchy touch to this combination along with the toasted sesame seeds.

Ingredients:
2 cups vinegared rice (*shari*) #1, see page 18
1 whole mackerel (½–¾ lb.(22.5–33.5 g) size)
1 tablespoon fresh young ginger, sliced into thin strips
1½ tablespoons salt pickled red *shiso* seed spikes (beefsteak plant)
10 fresh string beans
1½ tablespoons toasted white sesame seeds
salt, rice vinegar, sugar and *shoyu*

Method:
Prepare vinegared rice (*shari*). Put aside.
    Clean fish of innards. Slit fish from back side and remove bones. Wash carefully. Pat dry. Sprinkle with salt and set aside for 20–30 minutes. Rinse salt off with rice vinegar. Discard vinegar. Place fish in a non-metallic bowl. Mix together ½ cup rice vinegar (*su*), 3 tablespoons sugar and a dash of *shoyu*. Pour over fish. Marinate for 15 minutes. Remove skin. Slice into thin

strips. Fish flesh will be quite firm and color will turn greyish.

Rinse sliced fresh ginger in vinegar. Soak the pickled *shiso* in water and squeeze out the excess moisture. Cook fresh string beans in boiling water with a dash of salt for 5 minutes. Drain. Cut slantwise in thin slivers.

Mix prepared vinegared rice with marinated fish strips, ginger, pickled *shiso*, string beans and toasted sesame seeds.

Variation: 2 tablespoons sea urchin paste can be substituted for the shrimp. You can experiment and use anchovy paste although this would be a bit salty and you may wish to increase the sugar to offset the saltiness.

BARA-ZUSHI WITH *TAKUAN* AND *KAMABOKO*

Takuan is a yellowish naturally colored *daikon* radish pickle. It has a very pungent odor when the jar or package is opened but the flavor is nothing like the smell. It is oddly salty and sweet at the same time. Once the taste is acquired and your nose becomes accustomed to the "fragrance" you, too, will become an addict!

Ingredients:
2 cups vinegared rice (*shari*) #1, see page 18
1 piece *takuan*, 2 inches (5 cm) long
2 by 2-inch (5 × 5 cm) piece *kamaboko* (steamed fishcake), fresh or frozen
½ teaspoon rice vinegar (*su*)
2 tablespoons toasted white sesame seeds
½ sheet *nori* (laver seaweed) toasted

Method:
Prepare vinegared rice (*shari*). Put aside.

Cut *takuan* into shreds 1 inch (2.5 cm) long. Cut *kamaboko* into ¼-inch (6 mm) cubes. Sprinkle rice vinegar over the *kamaboko* to flavor and set aside.
Toast the white sesame seeds. Toss the prepared vinegared rice with *takuan*, *kamaboko* and toasted sesame seeds. Use a light mixing motion. Scoop onto plates. Garnish with toasted *nori* which has been torn into small pieces and green *shiso* leaves (beefsteak plant), if available.

Variation: In place of the *takuan* you could use *takana* (mustard leaves) or *nappa* (Chinese cabbage) pickles, chopped.

STUFFED
AND
FOLDED *SUSHI*

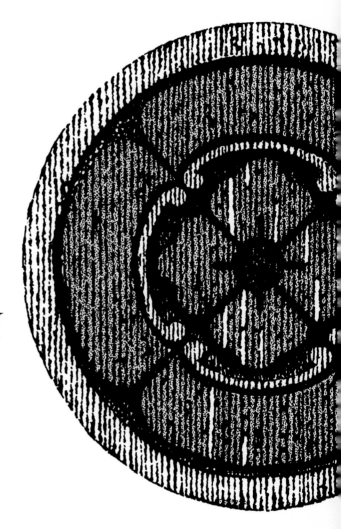

SUSHI IN OMELET SHEETS

This type of crêpe covered *sushi*, depending upon the shape of the wrapping method, derives a different name. Also regional colloquialism accounts for varied *sushi* titles. Basically these use an eggsheet in place of the conventional *nori* for wrapping. This *sushi* might be suitable for persons who are "uncertain" about *nori* (seaweed) taste.

FUKUSA-ZUSHI

Fukusa literally means a Japanese small crêpe scarf-type wrapper.

Ingredients:

1½ cups vinegared rice (*shari*) #1, see page 18
4 large eggs
Mixture A:
    2 tablespoons sugar
    dash salt
    2 teaspoons cornstarch dissolved in 1
       tablespoon water
oil for frying
1 oz.(30 g) dried *kampyo* (gourd shavings)
3–4 dried *shiitake* (black Japanese forest mushrooms), soak in warm water 20 minutes, squeeze excess moisture

2 tablespoons white sesame seeds, toasted
1½ sheets *nori*
Mixture B:
    1 cup *dashi*
    salt
    2½ tablespoons *shoyu* (soy sauce)
    3 tablespoons sugar
    1 tablespoon *mirin* (sweet Japanese rice wine)

Method:

Prepare the vinegared rice.

Beat eggs. Add Mixture A. Mix well. Strain through sieve. Heat square frying pan. Oil pan and remove excess. Pour ⅛ of the egg mixture into the hot pan. Make 8 eggsheets. Do not overcook. Refer to "How to make eggsheet" recipe, page 22.

Rub dried gourd shavings with salt. Rinse salt off in water. Cook in boiling water for 4–5 minutes. Squeeze out excess water from soaked mushrooms. Remove and discard stems. Fill a pan with Mixture B. Cook the *kampyo* and *shiitake* over medium heat until the juices have been absorbed. Cool *kampyo* and *shiitake*. Reserve half of the *kampyo* strips for ties and chop the balance along with the *shiitake* into ⅓-inch (8 mm) square pieces.

Toast white sesame seeds. Transfer sesame seeds to a piece of paper toweling. Cut across the seeds several times to release the good aroma and flavor. Toast the *nori* sheet on one side briefly. Rub to crumble.

Mix the vinegared rice with the chopped *kampyo*, *shiitake*, sesame seeds and crumbled *nori*. Divide into eight equal portions. Mold the rice mixture into balls with hands dampened with vinegar/water solution, see page 14.

Spread out the eggsheets. Place the rice mixture on each eggsheet. Fold one end of eggsheet over the rice mixture and fold up neatly as if you were to wrap a package. Place the end side up and tie the packet with the reserved half of the cooked *kampyo* strips.

CHAKIN-ZUSHI

The ingredients are the same as those for *fukusa-zushi* except for *oboro* mixture. The method of wrapping is different. This *sushi* simulates a draw string purse.

Spread out the eggsheet. Place the rice mixture on the eggsheet. Prepare *oboro* made by mashing fish or shrimp and adding some salt and sugar seasonings with a slight red color achieved by a few drops of food coloring. See recipe for *oboro* page 25.

Shape the edges of the eggsheet into scallops. Gather the edges together lightly leaving a top opening and loosely tie with blanched *mitsuba* (trefoil) or a stem portion of cooked spinach. You can place a small cooked shrimp over the mashed fish in the center where the eggsheet is tied together.

Garnish with a sprig of Japanese *kinomé* (*sansho*), a piece of parsley or watercress.

HAMAGURI-ZUSHI

This *sushi* has a clam shape—*hamaguri* specifies a variety of clam in Japan.

Ingredients:
2 cups vinegared rice (*shari*) #1, see page 18
6 eggs
Mixture A:
   3 tablespoons sugar
   dash salt
   1 tablespoon cornstarch dissolved in 1 tablespoon water
7 oz.(200 g) clam meat (fresh)
Mixture B:
   1 tablespoon *shoyu*
   1 tablespoon *saké*
12–15 leaves of *sansho* (prickly ash) or green *shiso* leaves

Method:
Prepare the vinegared rice.

Beat eggs. Add Mixture A. Mix well. Strain through a sieve. Heat a round frying pan until hot. Oil pan and remove excess. Pour egg mixture into the pan—about ¹⁄₁₂th. Make 12 eggsheets. Do not overcook. Put the clam meat in a strainer. Wash in salted water. Drain. Put clams in an oiled pan. Fry about 3 minutes. Season with Mixture B. Chop coarsely. Put aside.

Wash leaves from *sansho* or *shiso*. Drain. Chop coarsely. Mix vinegared rice with the cooked clams and leaves of *sansho* or *shiso*. Divide into 12 portions.

Spread out the eggsheets. Place vinegared rice mixture on ¼ section of each eggsheet. Fold eggsheet in four. Make a brand mark on the eggsheet with heated metal skewers. See the picture for mark placement.

Variations: Cooked seasoned *shiitake*, *kampyo*, *kamaboko* (steamed fishcake), toasted sesame seeds or whatever your imagination directs can be used in the rice mixture. One could even try chicken roast pieces, cooked crab or scallops, etc.

Hamaguri-Zushi

INARI-ZUSHI

INARI-ZUSHI

An intriguing mixture of ingredients with vinegared rice wrapped in fried soybean cakes (*agé*).

Approximately 30 balls:
3 cups vinegared rice (*shari*) #1, see page 18
15 *agé* (fried soybean cakes)
5 tablespoons *shoyu*
½ cup sugar
¼ teaspoon salt
1 tablespoon *mirin* (Japanese sweet rice wine)
2 tablespoons *shiso* pickles (salted beefsteak plant)
2 tablespoons white sesame seeds, toasted and chopped
2 oz.(50 g) lotus root, vinegared (available commercially pickled)

Method:
Prepare vinegared rice (*shari*).

Cut *agé* in half crosswise. Pat with a wooden pestle or rolling pin. This will help to make them easier to open up. Split the *agé* into pockets. Do this carefully.

Add *agé* to plenty of boiling water. Simmer over low heat for a few minutes to drain off excess oil.

Rinse *agé* in water Squeeze water out of *agé* one by one. Damp *agé* will not absorb the soup flavor very well.

Put *agé* in a cup of boiling water with *shoyu*, sugar, salt and *mirin*. Bring to a boil again. Reduce heat and cook until juices are absorbed. If necessary place a small saucer over the *agé* to keep below the water level. Squeeze the water out of the washed *shiso* pickles. Mix vinegared rice with *shiso*, sesame seeds and vinegared lotus roots (cut coarse pieces). Mold rice mixture into 30 balls. Before filling rice mixture into the seasoned *agé*, squeeze the *agé* lightly in palm of hands to prevent juices from soaking into the rice mixture. Fill rice mixture into the cooled *agé*. Firmly press the rice, however do it carefully so that *agé* does not tear. Do not pack in too much. It will get too big and oversized. There should be a loose appearance to the outer shell of *agé* covering. Not taut. Tuck opening flaps inward.

Interesting facts: ————————————————————————
Around the *Kansai* area hemp seed is mixed with the vinegared rice mixture. A bud of *kinomé* (Japanese pepper – prickly ash) is used in spring; *shiso* (beefsteak plant) is used in summer; a nutlet of *sansho* (Japanese pepper – prickly ash) is used in fall; a citron rind is added in winter. These enhance the *sushi* with rich and different flavors of the seasons.

KITSUNE-ZUSHI (Literally Fox *Sushi*)

This is *sushi* made with vinegared rice and seasoned ingredients mixed together stuffed in a flavored fried soybean cake (*aburagé* or *agé*). Also called *inari-zushi* (see glossary for other names). Foxes are mythically supposed to have guarded *Inari* shrines and the triangular shape looks like a fox (*kitsune*).

Ingredients:
3 cups vinegared rice (*shari*) #1, see page 18
10 *aburagé* (fried soybean cakes), rinsed in hot boiling water several times to remove excess oil
Mixture A:
    1 cup *dashi* (Japanese soup base)
    8 tablespoons sugar
    3 tablespoons *mirin* (Japanese sweet rice wine)
    3½ tablespoons *shoyu*
½ *gobo* (burdock root)
⅓ carrot, peeled
1½ tablespoons toasted white sesame seeds
1 tablespoon hemp seeds (optional)
oil
Mixture B:
    1½ tablespoons sugar
    1 tablespoon *shoyu*

Method:
Prepare vinegared rice (*shari*).

Place *agé* (fried soybean cakes) on a cutting board. Press the bean cakes with chopsticks like a rolling pin. Cut the *agé* in half crosswise on a diagonal. Open the cut side carefully and separate the inside to form a pocket. Place Mixture A in a pan. Bring to boiling point. Add the *agé*. A small saucer placed on top of *agé* keeps it down in the juices nicely. Cover. Cook over medium heat until the juices are absorbed. Put aside. Allow to cool in juices.

Wash *gobo* with a pot cleaner such as a plastic wiry one. Cut in half lengthwise. Then cut in paper thin diagonal slivers. Soak in cold water mixed with rice vinegar so the *gobo* will not oxidize and turn dark. Cut the carrot also in paper thin diagonal slivers. Heat some oil in a pan and fry *gobo* and carrot. Add Mixture B and simmer a few minutes. Remove from heat. Mix the cooked *gobo* and carrots, toasted sesame seeds and hemp seeds (optional) with the vinegared rice mixture. Divide into equal portions and shape into bite-size balls. Fill this rice mixture into the cooled seasoned *agé* pockets. Press rice lightly into the *agé* pockets since they tear easily. Shape into triangular shape as shown. Garnish with *beni shoga* (red pickled ginger). To vary: prior to filling turn some of the cooked *agé* inside out—the appearance is like a terry cloth *agé* . . . and proceed to fill.

The pronunciation is *ah-geh*—not age like your chronological age. If some rice filling is leftover serve in a dish garnished with pickled red ginger slivers.

NIGIRI-ZUSHI

▶

Sushi Restaurant
Edo Sushi Shop…
Aoyama Oh-Zushi, Tokyo

THE *SUSHI* RESTAURANT

The *sushi* shop entry way has a colorful *noren*—a short elongated cloth curtain sign with symbols/designs/characters thereon. You will see the character for *sushi* 鮨 in the center.

NIGIRI-ZUSHI

These *nigiri-zushi* can be excellent nibbling foods, hors d'oeuvres, picnic lunches or a whole meal. Simple to prepare. To become a true *sushi* maker takes years of experience and apprenticeship. But the majority of us are not attempting to become such a master so feel undaunted and try. You will achieve success in this culinary art form!

When eating the *nigiri-zushi* dip the top portion slightly in the *shoyu* (Japanese soy sauce) and bring it to your mouth. The topping should strike your tongue for optimum flavor. True *nigiri-zushi* is made so you can taste the topping and a bit of the *shari* (vinegared seasoned rice).

EDO-MAE (Shari)

This *shari* is the vinegared flavored steamed rice base used for preparing *nigiri-zushi*. *Edo* is the ancient name for the Tokyo area. The *tané* (topping) can be as varied as your imagination.

One uses this type of sour rice mixture for fresh raw fish toppings. Dabs of *wasabi* (Japanese horseradish) give the added zip. Naturally you can adjust the *shari* to your taste as you become more experienced.

Ingredients:
4½ cups short or medium grain rice (such as Kokuho rice, Calrose, etc.)
4½ cups water
¾ cups rice vinegar (*su*)
3¾ tablespoons sugar
1 tablespoon salt

Method:
Wash rice until water is clear. Transfer to a colander. Set aside and drain for 1 hour. Measure the water and add to the rice in a heavy pot or electric rice cooker. Bring to a boil, lower heat and allow rice to continue steaming for 15 minutes more with the cover on at all times. Remove from heat. Remove lid. Spread a clean cloth over the pot and recover. Allow to finish steaming without heat for 15 minutes. In the meanwhile mix the rice vinegar, sugar and salt together in a non–aluminum saucepan. Heat and stir to dissolve sugar. Put aside to cool. (Some people just mix these ingredients together, stir to dissolve and do not heat.) When the rice is properly steamed take a wooden spatula (*shamoji*) making cutting and turning motions with the rice. Do not smash the kernels.

Get a wooden flat bowl or large platter ready by rubbing the inside with a *tezu* (vinegar/water solution) dampened cloth, see page 14. Add the seasoned rice vinegar solution quickly to the hot rice. Keep fanning the hot rice mixture to remove as much moisture as possible and to cool more quickly. This will achieve a beautiful luster to the rice grains and the result will not be sticky or gummy. This takes about 10 minutes.

Try to keep the rice at room temperature. Keep the container covered with a clean cloth until you are ready to use the *shari*. It is at its best when there is a slight warmth to the rice still remaining since it can be molded easily. Do not refrigerate.

■ TO FORM THE *NIGIRI-ZUSHI*

Properly prepared vinegared rice should not crumble as you raise the rice ball to your mouth. The *nigiri-zushi* should stick together sufficiently to form a firm rice oval shape.

Prepare a damp cloth, *shari*, *tané* (toppings) and vinegared solution for dipping hands (*tezu* see page 14). Moisten fingers with the vinegared water. Place fish between the base of the fingers and the second joint of the left hand.

Shape the vinegared rice mixture into a ball with the right hand. Keep holding rice ball in the right hand and dab the *wasabi* on the first finger of the right hand. Place horseradish on fish slice which is in your left hand.

Place rice oval on fish. Press end of rice ball lightly with the thumb of the left hand. (Your left fingers will be cupped around the *sushi*.) Level rice top surface lightly with the right index finger.

Press ends of rice ball with the right thumb and index finger. Depress top of rice with index finger of right hand again. Turn the rice ball around with the thumb of the left hand and roll *sushi* into the right palm. Topping will be uppermost. Shape again. Press the end of the rice ball with the left thumb and index finger. Press topping of *sushi* lightly with two fingers of the left hand and once more mold the side edges of the *sushi* rice portion. Shape should be an elongated oval.

Variation: Simplified method of making *nigiri-zushi* is to dampen a cloth with vinegar/water solution. Squeeze out excess moisture. Place thereon the slice of topping such as fish, the *wasabi* on the fish slice and a rice ball on top. Grasp the dampened cloth up and twist to form a tight firm ball. Open the cloth carefully and "unload" the *nigiri-zushi* onto your plate . . . placing the rice portion on the bottom. Very unorthodox method but works for the inexperienced.

Garnish platter with a small mound of *wasabi* and *amazu shoga*.

■ TOPPINGS FOR *NIGIRI-ZUSHI* (bite-size *sushi*)

Choose your favorite fresh salt water raw fish, shellfish or roe. Here are just a few suggestions. As you "work" your way through this *sushi* book you will begin to see all the potential toppings—many which you never dreamed could be used for *sushi*.

maguro (tuna)	*unagi* (broiled eel)
hirame (flounder)	*gyoku* (omelet)
anago (conger eel)	fish roe
tekka (tuna wrapped in seaweed)	seabass
kohada (gizzard shad)	shrimp, cooked

raw thinly sliced beef steak fillet, if you are daring—similar to beef tartar
raw chicken breast, sliced thinly and marinated in lemon juice

The fresh raw fish is cut into a block the width of four fingers not counting the thumb. And then sliced 5/16 inch (8 mm) at an angle with 2 triangular pieces on each end. The end pieces are then butterflied to open into a "sort of slice" piece. These are normally sliced by the master chef while he holds the rice oval in one hand. We do not have to do that . . . since most of us would not be able to anyway!

NIGIRI-ZUSHI

This easy-to-do version of *nigiri-zushi* was devised by Ohmae Kinjiro, Master *Sushi* Chef of Japan. With his permission we share it with you.

1. Prepare *shari* (vinegared rice) in ping-pong ball size of about 2 tablespoons or 25–30 grams. This ball size is slightly larger than for *temaki-zushi*.
2. In your open left hand over the flattened fingers (not your palm) place the slice of raw fish (or whatever you choose).
3. Place some *wasabi* on the fish.
4. Then the rice ball.
5. Press the rice ball with the ball section of the palm of your left hand.
6.-7. Then flip over carefully so the ingredient portion becomes inverted in your palm showing the fish, in this instance, on top.
8. With the right thumb and index finger press firmly the 2 side edges of the *nigiri-zushi*.
9. With the index finger press down on the top surface of the fish.
10. Turn the *nigiri* portion clockwise.
11. Press lightly 1 or 2 times on this surface. Ready to serve without the difficult procedure of forming the rice into the proper *nigiri* shape with the right hand.

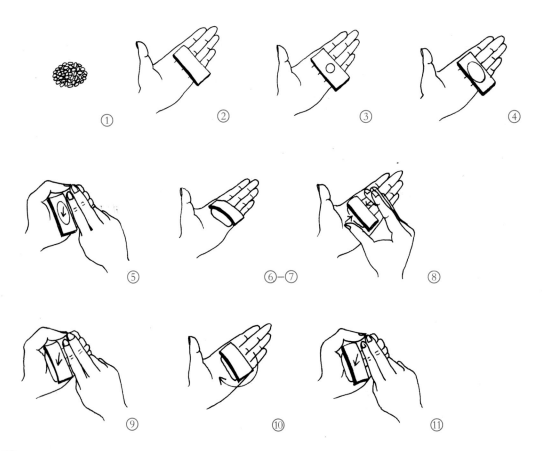

TEMAKI-ZUSHI

This simplified *temaki-zushi* preparation style is credited to Ohmae Kinjiro, Master *Sushi* Chef of Japan. With his permission we present it here.

1. For 5 persons with appetites of 10 pieces of *temaki-zushi* each prepare 50 ping-pong size balls of *shari* (vinegared rice) of about 2 tablespoons or 20–25 grams each.
2. Place these prepared balls in front of you on the work table.
3. Place the pre-cut toasted *nori* (laver) in your left open palm. Put a ball of *shari* in the center.
4. Apply a dab of *wasabi* using the tip of a chopstick or a small spatula.
5.-6. Next use chopsticks or small sugar tongs to place the *néta* (raw fish, egg, vegetable, etc.) on top of the rice ball and *wasabi*.
7. With the left thumb fold the *nori* sheet over to stick onto the rice.
8. With a slight rolling motion of the thumb and fingers, roll the *temaki-zushi* so the original fold will be at the bottom of your palm. See sketch.

   Your right hand will stay absolutely clean during the preparation process. The first few times may be difficult to get the knack of "how to roll"—after that it will be so easy!

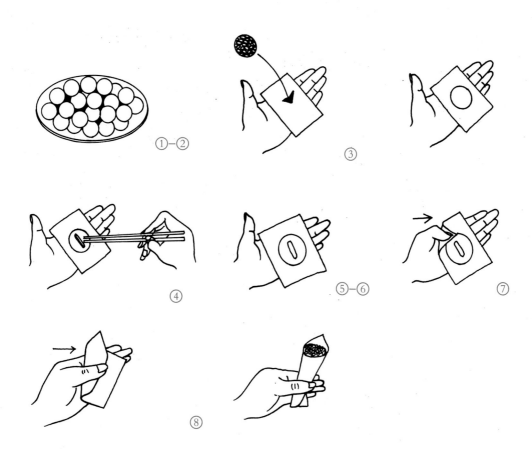

EDO-MAE NIGIRI-ZUSHI

Looks so easy to make but to become an expert could take years. Most of us are satisfied with being able to imitate. This is the *sushi* of the *sushi* bars—home style. The photo gives only a few selections. One can adapt to what is available in your area and what is your favorite.

Prepare 3 cups vinegared rice (*shari*) #3, see page 18.

To simplify preparation of the *tané* (topping) cut in advance. Generally in a *sushi* bar it is cut while the *sushi* chef has the rice oval in his left hand so the slice of the fresh raw fish, for instance, will be a new cut especially for that single *nigiri-zushi*. For home style we are not as experienced that we can juggle a rice ball in one hand and cut with the other, so we just do our best.

Plan on 12 slices of fresh raw tuna cut larger than the vinegared rice oval. It should overlap like the picture (the reddish colored fish slice). Place a dab of *wasabi* paste on the fish and put on top of the vinegared rice oval.

Another easy way to prepare for a beginner (a sort of cheater's method!) is to place the fish on a vinegar/water solution dampened cloth, see page 14. Then add the *wasabi* on the fish slice and place a vinegared rice oval on top. Bring the cloth up tightly to form a good firm ball of rice and fish inside. Release the cloth easily onto a plate, turning the *sushi* upright with the fish on the top part. The true way is to form the oval in your right hand as you will note on page 67.

Other *tané* (toppings) in picture are snowy white squid, egg omelet rectangle with a strip of *nori* enveloping the *sushi*, marinated vinegared mackerel and ark shell with *nori* strip tied around the *sushi*. A few slices of ginger garnish the platter of *sushi* in the picture.

Variations for *tané* (toppings)
Shrimps, scallops, abalone, octopus, red snapper, clams, broiled seasoned eel, thinly sliced raw beef with garlic powder sprinkled (similar to beef tartar) or raw chicken breast slices marinated in vinegar or lemon juice. Every cook has his special unlimited choices and favorites. A Western adaptation called "The California Roll" has become popular in the United States. It uses avocado and crab/shrimp, see page 118.

■ HOW TO EAT *NIGIRI-ZUSHI*

Pour some *shoyu* in a small sauce dish. Pick up the *nigiri-zushi* with your thumb and middle fingers. Your index finger will rest at the end of the *sushi*. Turn it over carefully while moving your fingers so the *tané* (topping) will be on the underside. This is when you dip the *tané* (topping) into the *shoyu*.

Do not get the *shoyu* on the rice portion. Carefully get it up to your mouth so the *tané* will land on your tongue. It sounds like quite a maneuver but once understood it isn't so difficult. And for the exquisite taste of *sushi* it is worth learning the right technique.

Sweet toppings such as conger eel, rolled egg and fresh fish seasoned with heavy *shoyu* flavored sauces should be eaten without *shoyu* dipping. If the smell of the fish and the sweetness of egg are left in your mouth you cannot taste the vinegared rice one after another. So you eat pickled ginger to freshen your mouth. Japanese rice wine (*saké*), Japanese green tea and beer are excellent liquids for partaking with a *sushi* meal.

71

OKONOMI-ZUSHI

The literal translation would be "as you like it *sushi*." A variation of *nigiri-zushi*—home style.

Prepare 3 cups vinegared rice (*shari*) #3, see page 18.

Topping ingredients
Fresh tuna, flounder, sea bream, cuttle fish, abalone, squid, octopus and cockle may be sliced according to the size of the rice ball. If using mackerel sprinkle salt on horse mackerel. Set aside for a few minutes. Rinse the salt off with rice vinegar. Discard this vinegar.

Eggsheet
Beat 3 eggs. Add 2 tablespoons sugar, ⅓ teaspoon salt and 3 tablespoons *dashi*. Mix well. Heat square frying pan. Oil pan and remove excess. Pour egg mixture into pan. Cook on low heat until the omelet is set. Do not brown excessively. Actually a slight tan appearance is acceptable. Cut according to the size of the rice shape.

Salmon roe and cod roe
Sprinkle some *saké* (Japanese rice wine) on the roe.
See page 133 for additional information about roe.

Canned crab, shrimp and clams
Remove from can and drain off juices. Sprinkle with rice vinegar (*su*).

Vegetables and other choices
Cucumbers and tomatoes may be cut for toppings or as something to munch on between bites. Canned asparagus, steamed fishcake (*kamaboko*), pickled vegetables (*tsukemono*), ham, chicken, pork roast, sausage, cheese, smoked salmon can be all sliced according to the rice ball size. The list is unlimited and again use whatever you like. Even bologna!

Americans are adventurous and dare to try innovative topping concoctions that a traditionalist would never consider. Here are a few examples: sliced fresh mushrooms dipped in rice vinegar with a thin lemon slice on top; slightly steamed broccoli or cauliflower with a *nori* strip; pickled eggplant; edible portions of artichoke scraped into a paste; slices of tangerines, bananas, strawberries, pears, apples or kiwi. An endless choice. Anything that could be put on a canapé would be fine except possibly very creamy cheese mixtures.

Seasonings
Toast the *nori* and cut in quarters (4 pieces) for this buffet-style *sushi*. In addition *nori* may be cut into 1-inch (2.5 cm) widths for thinly rolled *sushi*.

Condiments
Japanese horseradish (*wasabi*) is a green color and since the fresh is so very expensive we suggest you use the canned type. Dissolve the powdered *wasabi* with water to form a paste. Cover the container and allow to stand about 5 minutes for the flavor to develop. The taste of *wasabi* is so striking that for some they use the *sushi* language term of "*namida*" meaning tears.

Sweet pickled ginger (*amazu shoga*) or salted pickled ginger (*beni shoga*). These are available already pickled in your Asian food supply store. With ham, sausage and other meats you may wish to use a dissolved mustard paste rather than the *wasabi*. In Japan some people suggest using mayonnaise but I do not. To me as an American it destroys the true Japanese *sushi* flavor.

How to prepare
For salmon roe, cod roe, crab or other loose-type shellfish (such as chopped scallops) place on the vinegared rice ball after the ball has been surrounded by a strip of 1-inch (2.5 cm) wide *nori*. See *kakomi-zushi* page 96 for hints. Then put roe, etc. on top.

For *temaki-zushi* in this buffet style:
Put a quarter sized sheet of *nori* on your palm. Lay the vinegared rice ball on the *nori*. Place your favorite topping in the center. Wrap up by folding your hand. A piece of green *shiso* added along with the favorite topping adds zip.

As your hands become sticky wipe with a small dampened hand towel (*o-shibori*) placed at each diner's place.

For the final taste test
Place the favorite *sushi* ingredients on your vinegared rice ball with *wasabi* or mustard as is your desire. Dip topping in *shoyu* as you eat . . . getting not too much but just enough *shoyu* thereon to enjoy. Never on the rice portion.

Be sure to serve plenty of hot green tea with this *sushi* meal.

OSHI-ZUSHI AND BAR-SHAPED SUSHI

▶

Top: *Saba-Zushi*
Middle: *Tazuna-Zushi*
Bottom: *Oshi-Zushi*

OSHI-ZUSHI

This is an exotic set of *oshi-zushi* recipes—literally translated as press molded *sushi*. One can improvise if a mold is not available. Very much like an American sandwich.

Prepare 2 cups vinegared rice (*shari*) #3, see page 18. 3 × 8-inch (7.5 × 20 cm) mold required for each *oshi-zushi*. Or use a small shallow pyrex bread pan and extend the plastic wrap up the sides for easy unmolding.

OSHI-ZUSHI WITH FLOUNDER AND *KINOMÉ*

Ingredients:
1½ cups cooked prepared vinegared rice (*shari*)
3 oz.(90 g) sliced flounder
6 leaves *kinomé* or substitute watercress
½ sheet *nori*, toasted (3 × 8-inch (7.5 × 20 cm) sheet)
plastic wrap

Method:
Moisten mold with vinegar/water solution, see page 14. Cut a piece of plastic wrap and place in bottom of mold. Lay the flounder with the leaves on top. Next place half of the rice mixture. Level with finger tips. Lay the toasted *nori* on it. Top with remaining rice mixture. Press down with a lid. Unmold. Cut into 6 pieces.

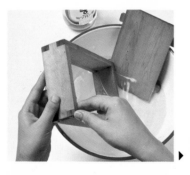  

OSHI-ZUSHI WITH SHRIMP AND ROLLED OMELET

Ingredients:
1½ cups cooked prepared vinegared rice (*shari*)
3 cooked shrimp, shelled and butterflied
rolled omelet

Method:
Line a piece of plastic wrap on bottom of dampened mold. Place shrimp and rolled omelet on it. Top with vinegared rice mixture. Press down. Unmold. Cut into serving pieces.

OSHI-ZUSHI WITH CONGER EEL AND CUCUMBER

Ingredients:
1½ cups cooked prepared vinegared rice (*shari*)
1 broiled conger eel or canned *unagi no kabayaki*
¼ cucumber, sliced lengthwise strips

Method:
Line a piece of plastic wrap on bottom of mold. Place conger eel and cucumber on it. Top with vinegared rice mixture. Press down. Unmold. Cut into serving pieces.

OSHI-ZUSHI WITH SALMON AND NORI IN HAKATA STYLE

Ingredients:
1½ cups cooked prepared vinegared rice (*shari*)
1 piece salted salmon or smoked salmon slices
1 tablespoon *sake* (Japanese rice wine)
½ sheet *nori*, toasted (3 × 8-inch (7.5 × 20 cm) piece)

Method:
Freeze salted salmon briefly to firm the flesh. Remove the skin and bones. Cut on a diagonal. Sprinkle with *sake*. Marinate for 15 minutes. Wipe off any excess moisture. Line a piece of plastic wrap on bottom of mold. Place salmon on the bottom. Lay half of the rice mixture on it. Level with finger tips. Place *nori* next. Top with the balance of the rice mixture. Press down with a lid. Unmold. Cut in serving pieces.

▶
Molded *Sushi*:
Strawberries and
Kiwi Fruits

MOLDED HAM *SUSHI*

A modern version with an American influence. One could use any leftover roast such as pork, beef or poultry. This *sushi* has a "party" look to it.

Ingredients:
2 cups vinegared rice (*shari*) #3, see page 18
10 oz.(300 g) sliced ham (thinly sliced sandwich style is ideal)
2 tablespoons *saké* (Japanese rice wine)
1 teaspoon sugar
bamboo leaves, orchid flowers or aspidistra leaves, if available
sweet pickled ginger (*amazu shoga*)

Method:
Prepare vinegared (*shari*) rice. Set aside.

Mix the *saké* and sugar until dissolved. Set aside. Line an 8-inch (20 cm) cake pan with plastic wrap. Place ham on the bottom of the pan arranged into the petals of a flower as shown in the picture. Sprinkle half of the *saké*/sugar mixture on the ham. Pat ½ of the cooled vinegared rice (*shari*) mixture on the ham evenly. Press down firmly so the mixture will pack slightly and not be too loosely grained.

Place the remaining ham slices on top of the rice layer. Sprinkle the balance of the *saké*/sugar mixture on the ham again. Repeat the rice layering with the remaining vinegared rice. Spread level and press down firmly with fingers so the rice will be compact.

Wash and drain orchid flower, aspidistra leaves or *sasa* (large bamboo leaves) whatever is available. Line a platter and invert the cake pan of molded *sushi* thereon.

Top center either with sweet pale pink pickled ginger slices (*amazu shoga*) or red pickled ginger (*beni shoga*), sliced and formed to simulate a flower. Serve by cutting into 5–6 wedges. If regular cake pan is very shallow I suggest a spring form cake pan or make two separate layers and place one on top of the other.

BAR-SHAPED *SUSHI*

SHIME-SABA (Vinegared Mackerel)

Fresh mackerel is relatively inexpensive compared to some other fishes. And it is often considered a fish not suited to the tastes of the elegant gourmet. However once you have "open-minded" yourself to try a really fresh mackerel you will probably change your mind. Aside from preparing mackerel in this manner one can prepare it as *shio-saba* (Japanese salted broiled mackerel) and that is something that delights more gourmets, especially the nice fatty Autumn mackerel that comes from Japan waters.

This recipe is raw mackerel soaked in a seasoned vinegar solution and has many uses. One can eat this as vinegared mackerel by itself; it can be the base for *saba-zushi* page 86 or it can be combined in a salad-type dish.

Ingredients:
1 mackerel (1 lb. (450 g) or more)
salt
rice vinegar (*su*) for rinsing
1 piece dried *kombu* (kelp) twice as long as mackerel
Mixture A:
    ½ cup rice vinegar (*su*)
    2 tablespoons *mirin* (Japanese sweet rice wine)
    several slices fresh ginger root
Vegetables and condiments:
    1 cucumber
    2-inch (5 cm) slice *daikon* (Japanese white radish)
    grated fresh ginger, *shoyu* and lemon rind slivers

Method:
Fillet fish and remove bones but leave skin intact. Cover the bamboo or plastic strainer with salt. Place the mackerel side by side. Cover the surface of the mackerel with salt. Set aside for 4–5 hours in a cool place. Cover with a plastic wrap if desired. Rinse the salt off of the salted mackerel with some rice vinegar. Discard this rinsing vinegar.

Place dried *kombu* on a plate. Fill the plate with Mixture A. Soak the salted mackerel with the meat side down in the seasoned vinegar solution with the *kombu* at bottom and on top. Cover tightly with a plate on top. Press down with weights such as a clean brick covered with a plastic wrap. Marinate for 2–3 hours.

Use a tweezer and pick out the small bones on the blood veins. Remove the thin skin from the head portion of the fish working toward the tail end. Serve sliced on dishes. Or use as a base for the *saba-zushi* recipe.

Cut *daikon* and cucumber into thin slices. Marinate in 2 tablespoons rice vinegar and 1 tablespoon sugar with a dash of salt. Mix. These vegetables can be used as edible garnishes for the marinated mackerel. Serve with condiments of grated fresh ginger root, *shoyu* and lemon rind slivers.

SHIME-SABA

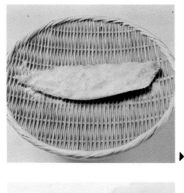

SABA-ZUSHI

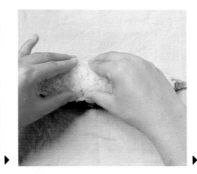

SABA-ZUSHI (*Sushi* with Vinegared Mackerel)

This *sushi* is for tasting after a person has learned real *sushi* flavors. It is a very sophisticated acquired taste . . . and relished!

Ingredients:
1 large vinegared mackerel or 2 small mackerels (see preparation
    method *shime-saba* page 84)
3 cups rice (short grain) such as Kokuho or Calrose.
3¼ cups water
1 tablespoon *saké*
1 piece dried *kombu* (kelp) 5 inches (12.5 cm) long
Mixture A:
    4½ tablespoons rice vinegar (*su*)
    2 teaspoons salt
    2 or 2½ tablespoons sugar

Condiments:
1 tablespoon grated fresh ginger root
1 tablespoon grated lemon peel (optional)

Method:
Cook rice mixture in a covered heavy pan and when it comes to a boil, remove the *kombu*. Turn down the heat and continue to cook the rice for 20 minutes. The steam will complete the cooking process after the heat source has been shut off. Set aside to steam, covered, 15 minutes with no heat. Transfer the cooked rice to a clean wooden platter or bowl. Do not use a metal bowl if possible. Never aluminum since the acid from the vinegar will attack it. Sprinkle the vinegar solution (Mixture A) over the rice. Use a fan to cool the rice rapidly and allow the moisture to evaporate while you constantly fold and turn the rice kernels carefully with the vinegar solution. If you have a wooden *shamoji* (rice paddle) all the better. Do not mash the kernels. Put aside to cool with a dish cloth on top.

Slice the meatiest portions of mackerel in a slantwise position. This will even out the fish piece (not too thick one place and too thin in another). Be careful not to cut through the skinned side since you wish the appearance to be completely as if the fish were still whole and intact. See picture.

Squeeze a clean cloth in vinegar/water solution, see *tezu* page 14. Spread this cloth out on the *sudaré*. Shape a quarter of the rice mixture into an oblong shape. Place on the cloth. Wrap it tightly with the cloth and *sudaré*. Release the *sudaré*.

Now lay a plastic wrap on the *sudaré*. Put the molded rice block back in the center of the plastic wrap. Place grated fresh ginger and if desired the grated fresh lemon peel on the flesh portion. The vinegared mackerel with the skinned side up on the rice mixture is how this *saba-zushi* should look. Wrap in plastic wrap. Shape again with the *sudaré*. Press down. Set aside. Cut when ready to serve. Do not place in the refrigerator. In the event you should have some leftover wrap completely with foil and put in refrigerator for no more than one day. However serve it at room temperature. Refrigeration hardens the rice kernels of any *sushi* mixture. The ideal is to consume it the day it is prepared. Usually it will disappear quickly in the hands of the diners!

TAZUNA-ZUSHI

A uniquely designed *sushi* patterned with assorted diagonal strips similar to a rein pattern—*tazuna*. One could vary the topping using what is available. Versatile *sushi* idea.

WITH SHRIMP AND CUCUMBERS

Ingredients:
1 cup vinegared rice #3, see page 18.
3 fresh raw medium to large size shrimp with shells
½ cucumber
salt and rice vinegar (*su*)

Method:
Prepare the vinegared rice (*shari*). Put aside.

Remove veins from shrimp. Spear a skewer from the tail through the opposite end to prevent curling. Put shrimps in boiling water with salt. Cook 3–4 minutes. Remove skewers and after cooled, peel. Split in half vertically leaving the back portion intact. Sprinkle with rice vinegar (*su*).

Rub whole, unpeeled cucumber with salt lightly. Allow to stand about 5 minutes. Wash with water. Slice vertically in thin slices. Sprinkle a dash of salt to make the cucumber pliable.

Mold vinegared rice into a large oblong shape. Dampen a linen or cotton cloth square with vinegar/water solution (*tezu*), see page 14. Squeeze out excess moisture. Place shrimp and cucumber side by side on an angle as pictured. Put the vinegared rice block on top. Roll up with the cloth to shape, keeping the cloth intact. Cover with a *sudaré* (bamboo mat). Press down firmly to mold shape. Remove *sudaré* and cloth carefully and place the *sushi* on a serving dish. Cut with a sharp knife moistened with vinegar/water solution. Serving slices should be about 4–5 per block.

WITH ROAST PORK AND CHEESE

Definitely a Western adaptation of *sushi*—an ideal way for leftover roasts.

Ingredients:
1 cup vinegared rice (*shari*) #3, see page 18
3–4 slices lean roast pork (or substitute chicken, beef or turkey)
3–4 slices cheese
a small cucumber
salt

Method:
Prepare the vinegared rice (*shari*). Allow to cool.

Cut roast and cheese into 1-inch (3 cm) width slices. Cut cucumber thinly. Salt to soften cucumber.

Dampen a linen or cotton cloth as per previous recipe using shrimp and cucumber. Observe picture for details. Proceed in the same manner. Slice to serve.

WITH FIVE COLORS

This *sushi* offers many possible variations as one discovers the type of ingredients which go best with *sushi*.

Ingredients:
1 cup vinegared rice (*shari*) #3, see page 18.
1 or 2 *kisu* (smelts)
2 oz.(50 g) fish fillet with white meat such as halibut or
    turbot to be used for *oboro* (mashed fish)
2 dried *shiitake* (black Japanese forest mushrooms), soak in warm water
    for 20 minutes, squeeze out excess moisture
2-inch (5 cm) piece of carrot
5 or 6 fresh string beans
salt
oil
shoyu (soy sauce)
saké
rice vinegar (*su*), sugar and red food coloring

Method:
Prepare the vinegared rice (*shari*). Put aside.

Clean the *kisu* and remove the bones. Sprinkle with salt. Set aside for a few minutes until salt is dissolved. Marinate in rice vinegar for 5 minutes. Slice in strips.

Remove skin and bones from fish fillet if necessary. Chop. Add a dash of *saké*. Cook briefly in a hot oiled pan. Remove to a *suribachi* (Japanese style mortar for pulverizing foods). Mash. Put back in pan. Add dash of salt with 2 teaspoons sugar and a few drops of red food coloring. Continue to cook over low heat until dry and flaky. This should not take too long. Do not scorch.

Cut off stems of soaked *shiitake* and discard. Slice thinly. Add 2 tablespoons water, 1 tablespoon sugar and 2 teaspoons *shoyu*. Simmer and stir until liquid is absorbed. Shred carrots. Put in pan. Add 1 tablespoon water, 2 teaspoons sugar and dash salt. Cook about 3 minutes until liquid is absorbed.

Cut string beans French-cut in long thin strips. Cook in boiling water with dash of salt for 4–5 minutes.

Squeeze out a cloth dampened with vinegar/water solution (*tezu*). Place on top of *sudaré* (bamboo mat). Pat a 10-inch (25 cm) square of plastic wrap on the cloth. Place the prepared ingredients (smelt, mashed fish, *shiitake*, carrot and beans) side by side in a diagonal pattern as shown in photo (P.91).

Mold the vinegared rice into a large oblong shape. Place shaped rice on top of the diagonally placed ingredients. Roll up firmly with the help of the cloth and the *sudaré* (bamboo mat) to compress the shape of the *sushi*. Remove *sudaré*. Cut the bar of *sushi* with a sharp knife in 5 pieces with the plastic wrap still attached.

Remove plastic wrap carefully so the pattern will not be disturbed.

Variation: In place of mashed fish sweet flavored scrambled egg could be used. Again imagination should give you some refreshing ideas!

Roast Pork and Cheese

Five Colors

MORE *SUSHI* RECIPES

▶

Mini-Mini-*Zushi*

A tantalizing assortment array of miniature nibbling *sushi*. Fairly easy to prepare at home. They will be most attractive served on lacquered trays. The *sushi* is made expressly smaller in proportion. These make fabulous appetizers.

Prepare vinegared rice (*shari*) #3, see page 18 as basic *shari* for all these recipes.

1. Self-service *Nigiri-Zushi*

Select raw fish. Use a dampened *sushi* mold or not having that make a long roll with the vinegared rice (*shari*) dampening your hands first with a solution of rice vinegar/water (see *tezu* page 14). Cut into large slices from the roll about ¾ inch (3.7 cm) wide.

Place tuna, ark shell or whatever fresh fish assortment is available (cut larger than the rice portions) on a small serving tray. Make an attractive mound of the raw fish. Add a smaller mound of *wasabi* on the side. To eat take a piece of the molded vinegared rice (*shari*) and top with your choice of fish plus add a dab of *wasabi* to the fish. The point is to have more topping with just a bit of vinegared rice taste. Each diner picks out what topping is desired with the rice ball. Very suitable for individual servings also.

2. Canapé-*Zushi*

Refer to *kakomi-zushi* recipe, page 96.

Form the vinegared rice (*shari*) into an oval shape about 1½ inches (3.7 cm) long. Cut toasted *nori* in strips about 1 by 7 inches (2.5 × 17.5 cm). Wrap around the oval of rice. Seal end of overlapping *nori* strip with a smashed rice kernel. Top with a dab of *wasabi* (Japanese horseradish), vinegared egg (recipe follows) and a scoop of salmon roe.

Vinegared Egg: Mash 1 hard boiled egg. Add 1 teaspoon rice vinegar (*su*), 1 tablespoon sugar and a dash of salt. Put in a dry heated frying pan. Mix well while stirring over medium heat for about 1 minute. Push this thick mixture through a coarse sieve over half of the rice oval.

3. *Chakin-Zushi*

Make your usual thin eggsheet.

Cut a 3-inch (7.5 cm) square. Make a vinegared rice (*shari*) ball about 1½ inches (3.7 cm) in diameter. Place in the center of the eggsheet square. Wrap the rice ball by bringing all four corners to the center. Tie with a strip of flavored *kampyo* strip. Garnish with *kinomé* or watercress sprig.

4. Rolled Egg *Sushi*

Prepare a thin eggsheet with cornstarch added to hold shape better, see page 22. Place eggsheet on *sudaré*. Place *sushi* rice (*shari*) on the eggsheet in the section closest to you leaving about 1 inch (1.5 cm) without rice on it. Place *mitsuba* (trefoil) in the center left to right or substitute cooked spinach or string beans. Roll up carefully. The overlap of eggsheet will be about 1 inch (2.5 cm). Carefully set the roll on the seam edge to "firm up." Slice in 1-inch (2.5 cm) widths as pictured for serving.

5. Flower-Shaped *Sushi*

Using a *sushi* mold, dampen it, press *sushi* rice into it. Spread cod roe, other choice roe or mashed flavored shrimp (*oboro*) on top. Apply a piece of plastic film wrap over the top. Place the lid over the mass. Press down. Cut with a flower-shaped cutter. Garnish with boiled egg yolk pressed through a sieve. If finding a *sushi* mold is difficult substitute by pressing vinegared rice into a flat rectangular pan over a dampened cloth lined with plastic wrap approximately 1¼ inches (3 cm) high. Top with cod roe or whatever you desire. Put a plastic film wrap overall and press down with a pan or other flat surface. Remove wrap and cut into squares or diamond-shaped *sushi*. Garnish with sieved boiled egg yolk.

6. Inari-Zushi

Prepare *agé* (fried soybean cake – *tofu*), see page 47, with seasonings. Cut on diagonal. Turn half of the *agé* inside out. The *agé* will have a "terry cloth" look. Cook as directed in the *inari-zushi* recipe. Lightly squeeze out the juice. Mix shredded *yuzu* (citron) peel or substitute lemon peel with the vinegared rice (*shari*). Stuff lightly into the cooked seasoned *agé*. Shape like a cone pyramid. Top with toasted white sesame seeds.

7. Sugata-Zushi

Devein shrimp and thread a toothpick lengthwise from the head to the tail. Cook 3 minutes with 2 tablespoons water and 1 teaspoon *saké* until shrimp turns red. Cool, remove picks. Remove shells leaving only the tails intact. Slit on the underside of the shrimp leaving the top side of the shrimp uncut. Open flat. Spread a dab of *wasabi* inside the shrimp bodies. Place on top of a finger-shaped oval of vinegared rice (*shari*).

8. Oharamé

Toasted *nori* is made up into very thin cigar-like rolls with vinegared rice. Three of these rolls are tied together with a sash made from a thin eggsheet.

Check index for more detailed preparation instructions for each type of *sushi*.

Kakomi-Zushi (Canapé-*Zushi*)

Chakin-Zushi

KAKOMI-ZUSHI

Kakomi-zushi can be literally translated as encircling the *sushi* . . . other names for this special shaped *sushi* are *Gunkan maki* (battleship wrap) or *Funamori* (boat wrap).

This style of *sushi* is easily prepared and could be adapted to a "do-it-yourself" party. Each rice ball is formed (about 1-inch in diameter) into a finger shape surrounded by lightly toasted *nori* (laver seaweed).

Topping is placed on top. It is an ideal way for any kind of filling which would not adapt well to *nigiri* or *maki-zushi*—basically because the topping is in small pieces such as salmon roe, etc. Although one can use it as a simpler method to make rather than the *nigiri-zushi* which requires a certain amount of skill to form the firm rice oval. This *sushi* has a wrapper of *nori* to hold the rice with slight support.

For about 20 pieces of *Kakomi-zushi*:
Ingredients:
Prepare 2 cups vinegared rice (*shari*) #3, see page 18
Suggested toppings:
sea urchin (*uni*)
cooked shrimp, butterfly-cut or chopped coarsely
cooked small bay shrimp
bay scallops
cucumber, shredded in ½-inch (12 mm) thick strips
salmon roe
dried young sardines
oboro (mashed shrimp or white fish seasoned and colored pinkish-red—see glossary) ·
3½ sheets *nori* (laver seaweed)

Method:
Toast *nori* over heat briefly on one side. Cut vertically into six strips. (3½ sheets would yield 21 strips. Take one of those strips and cut into 8 thin strips. These are to be used as fasteners.)

Divide vinegared rice into 20 small portions. Mold into elongated shapes as shown. Wrap a strip of *nori* around the rice ball sticking the end with a kernel of smashed rice. The rice mixture should not overflow the *nori* wrapper.

Cut your topping ingredients to fit the shape or spoon on as may be the case. Choose about 5 different kinds of toppings. The dried sardines and cucumber ones are "fastened" with a piece of sliced tiny *nori* strip in picture.

The scallops, shrimps and cucumber toppings can be flavored with a few drops *shoyu* on top of filling if desired. Place *sushi* on a plate first however before adding *shoyu* drops. Improvise your own topping much as you do a sandwich filling.

Variations: Scrambled eggs, canned tuna (drained), *unagi no kabayaki* (seasoned eel), pickles, vegetables, etc. This is an intriguing and different way for you and your guests to partake of *sushi* with some of the *sushi* bar atmosphere right in your home.

TEMAKI-ZUSHI (Hand Rolled *Sushi*)

A very adaptive modern buffet-style *sushi* idea. Use ingredients that suit you. It will entail very little effort for you as the cook. Let your guests choose their favorite combinations and "roll" their own with their "clean" hands (Japanese word for hand is *té*). Be sure to "serve" everyone a steamy hot *o-shibori* (hand towel) tightly rolled cigar-shaped to wipe hands before the meal. This *sushi* style will be even more of a delicacy since each person can select what he prefers and "try" making his own *sushi*!

Ingredients:
Prepare 3 cups vinegared rice (*shari*) #1, see page 18
Cut the following 5 ingredients below in vertical strips 3½ inches (3.7 cm) long by ¼ inch
 (6 mm) square
2 cucumbers
4 pieces cheese
6 oz.(180 g) cooked ham
2 eggs made into a thick sweet omelet, see page 23
4 slices fresh raw sea bass or other salt water fish such as tuna, halibut, gizzard shad
6 sheets *nori* (laver seaweed), toasted one side over heat source, cut into quarters
1 fresh cod roe, if available, (optional) slit skin and open, chop. Sprinkle with a bit of
 lemon juice and pound into a paste
7–8 fresh green *shiso* leaves, chopped or substitute several sprigs of watercress. *Shiso*
 (beefsteak plant) gives a delightful aromatic flavor that goes beautifully with *sushi*
2 large *umeboshi* (pickled Japanese red plums), mashed and mixed with ½ can tuna,
 drained

Method:
Arrange all the ingredients as shown. This picture is suggestive only and you can substitute freely with what ingredients you have on hand. Other suggestions are crab meat, bits of roast chicken or meat, canned eel, sliced smoked salmon or any of the roes that are now on the market. See index for information on roes.

 Put a piece of *nori* on your hand and top with a spoonful of vinegared rice and your favorite filling combination of fillings.

 Grasp the *nori* to close the roll completely. You do not cut this *sushi*. It can be dipped in *shoyu* and bites taken from the miniature roll. (Roll can be ice-cream cone-shape or rolled like cigar-shape). I have been served this *temaki-zushi* with a leaf of *shiso* peeking out of the open end of the *nori* roll combined with fresh tuna and a dab of *wasabi*. Just a wee bit of *shari* was used. It was delicious! Don't forget the large cups of green tea to go with the *sushi* and some *amazu shoga* for the cleansing of your palate between bites.

FOUR VARIATIONS OF ROLLED *SUSHI*

SUSHI WRAPPED WITH PICKLED VEGETABLE LEAF

The pickled leaf (*tsukemono*) has just enough saltiness and intensifies the filling taste. The entire concoction harmonizes well with the vinegared rice.

Ingredients:
Prepare 1 cup vinegared rice (*shari*) #1, see page 18
6 leafy *tsukemono* (salted pickled greens, such as
    takana—mustard greens as pictured)
1 oz. (30 g) pork
2 oz. (60 g) bamboo shoots
Seasonings:
    1 tablespoon *shoyu*
    2 teaspoons *saké* (Japanese rice wine)
    1 teaspoon sugar
oil for frying

Method:
Divide the vinegared rice into 3 portions. Rinse the pickled vegetable in running water. Drain well. Squeeze out the water. Flatten out. Put aside.

Slice pork and bamboo into strips. Mix seasonings with the pork and bamboo strips. Heat a small skillet. Swish a little oil in the hot skillet. Fry the pork/bamboo mixture until juices have evaporated.

Lay out the leaf of *tsukemono* on the *sudaré*. Place the vinegared rice mixture on it. Leave about ½-inch (12 mm) margin at edge with no rice. Put the cooked mixture down the center of the rice. Wrap up with *sudaré*. Let stand a few minutes to firm the shape. Slice to serve.

Variation:
Use chicken breast slices and seasoned carrot strips. There are no rules to making this kind of *sushi*!

▶

Top: *Temaki-zushi*
Middle Right: *Sushi* with eggsheet
Middle Left: *Sushi* wrapped with pickled vegetable leaf
Bottom: *Sushi* wrapped in tangle flakes

TEMAKI-ZUSHI

This manner of serving the *sushi* allows one to form his own serving with the advantage of consuming it while the toasted *nori* (laver seaweed) is still crunchy. The best aroma of the fragrant *nori* flavor is savored this way.

Ingredients:
1½ cups vinegared rice (*shari*) #1, see page 18
2 sheets *nori* (laver seaweed)
2 oz.(60 g) fresh squid mantle (white cone body portion)
1½ tablespoons toasted white sesame seeds
2 teaspoons salted sea urchin (optional)
salt

Method:
Toast *nori* sheets over a gas or electric burner for a few seconds. Cut each sheet in 4 pieces quarter-wise. Remove the skin from the squid. Parboil in salted boiling water for a minute or so. Cool. Slice in 2-inch (5 cm) strips.

Toast sesame seeds in hot dry pan. Pulverize seeds to get the best aroma. Mix sesame seeds with the squid and salted sea urchin, if used. To pulverize sesame seeds use a mortar/pestle or to be truly authentic use a *suribachi* set. (A small bowl with coarse markings inside so seeds will be crushed when pressed with a small stick).

Divide the vinegared rice into 8 portions. Place the toasted *nori* in your hand. Put one portion of vinegared rice on the *nori* spreading it out. Put the filling mixture down the center. Close up your hand, shape and the *sushi* will be wrapped in *nori* nicely. Eat as soon as possible for the best taste.

SUSHI WRAPPED IN TANGLE FLAKES

This uses shaved seaweed (sea vegetable) in another form. This displays a very versatile nutritious product of the seas, and how the Japanese have utilized what was available within their shores.

Ingredients:
Prepare 2 cups vinegared rice (*shari*) #1, see page 18
2 oz.(60 g) tangle flakes (*oboro kombu*)
20 shrimp (medium size)
Marinade:
    ⅓ cup rice vinegar (*su*)
    3 tablespoons sugar
    1 teaspoon *shoyu*

Method:
Devein shrimp without peeling off shells. Insert a wooden skewer through the body to keep the shrimp straight while boiling. Cook in boiling water for about 3 minutes or less. Cool. Remove shells. Soak in marinade mixture for 30 minutes. Cut in strips.

Divide the vinegared rice into 6 portions. Lay a vinegar/water dampened cloth on the *sudaré*. Place vinegared rice on it. Put the marinated shrimp in the center. Roll with the *sudaré*. Remove the cloth. Place the rice mixture onto tangle flakes and roll rice like a rolling pin over the tangle flakes. Cut into slices to serve.

SUSHI WITH EGGSHEET

Many varied ingredients combine to give good flavor to this creation.

Ingredients:
Prepare 1 cup vinegared rice (*shari*) #1, see page 18
3 eggs
5 medium-size shrimp
2 tablespoons rice vinegar (*su*)
1 dried *shiitake* (black Japanese forest mushroom), soak in warm water for 15 minutes,
    squeeze out excess water
1 bamboo shoot, cut in shreds ¼-inch (6 mm) long
several strips dried *kampyo* (gourd shavings)
1 small carrot, peeled and cut in shreds ¼-inch (6 mm) long
a few spinach leaves
Seasonings:
    1 tablespoon *shoyu*
    1 tablespoon sugar
    1 tablespoon *mirin*

Method:
Make 3 eggsheets. Beat eggs together and fry on lightly oiled square skillet to form 3×6-inch (7.5×15 cm) squares. Fry only on one side. Put aside.

Do not peel shrimp. Devein. Put a skewer through body to hold shape. Boil in water for 3 minutes. Peel off shells. Chop coarsely. Soak in rice vinegar for 15 minutes. Drain before use.

Chop *shiitake* in pea-size pieces. Rub dried *kampyo* shavings with salt. This will soften shavings prior to cooking. Rinse. Slice into ¼-inch (6 mm) lengths. Cook *shiitake*, *kampyo*, bamboo shoots and carrots in a little water for about 3 minutes.

Pour seasonings over above cooked vegetables and stir. Cook down about 2 minutes to evaporate liquid.

Quickly blanch spinach leaves with boiling water and a dash of salt (just long enough to soften and retain the sharp green color).

Mix vinegared rice with the above seasoned shrimp and vegetables. (Do not include the eggsheet in this mixture).

Lay on *sudaré* the eggsheet with the browned fried portion on top so that the part you cannot now see will become the outside when you have completed the rolling process. The finished eggroll will appear completely yellow without tan frying marks.

Lightly put one-third of the vinegared rice mixture on the eggsheet leaving about ¾-inch (18 mm) without any rice on it on the furthest part from you. Roll up firmly away from you overlapping eggsheet at the end around itself. It is almost impossible to "glue" this together where it overlaps. Therefore place the rolled up *sushi* with the overlapping portion downward on the seam so it will not fall apart until ready to serve. Cut and place the slices upright as shown in the picture. All these "sticking," rolling, etc. processes of *sushi* making take a learning period and experience but again practice makes perfect so keep tying!

HANA-ZUSHI WITH LEAVES

These are a set of recipes utilizing the abundance of natural green leaves which can be used in season along with the *sushi* for an attractive presentation. Choose however only the leaves of plants which are suggested since there are some plants in nature which are toxic to humans.

SUSHI WITH CHERRY LEAVES AND BLOSSOMS

This unique recipe uses the salted cherry blossoms sold during the spring season. Try also these specially prepared blossoms in a tea cup with hot water to make an elegant ceremonial tea —delicate in taste and exquisite in appearance.

Ingredients:
1 cup vinegared rice (*shari*) #3, see page 18
10 small sea bream covered with bamboo leaves but if this special pickled
    form of fish is unavailable use fresh sea bream and after cutting diagonally, sprinkle with
    salt. Put aside for 15 minutes
cherry blossoms pickled in salt (double cherry blossoms prepared and sold in
    small packets)
rice vinegar (*su*)
10 cherry leaves, washed, drained and salted or use already salt-pickled leaves

Method:
Prepare vinegared rice (*shari*). Put aside.
   Remove bones from sea bream. Rinse off in rice vinegar. Discard vinegar.
   Rinse salt off of cherry blossoms in water. Discard excess water. Drain. Divide vinegared rice mixture into 10 equal portions. Place sea bream with the skin side down on the vinegar/water dampened cloth. Lay the cherry blossoms on each side of the fish slice. Place the rice ball on top. Wrap in the dampened cloth. Bring edges of cloth together and squeeze tightly to form a firm ball shape. Remove the cloth. Place a leaf from the cherry tree around the rice ball as pictured.
   If salted leaves are not available you can salt some for yourself. Sprinkle on cleaned, damp leaves some salt and allow to stand for a few hours to soften. Wipe off and use. Cherry leaves are also traditionally used in Japan for special sweet rice cakes.

SUSHI WITH CAMELLIA LEAVES

Ingredients:
1 cup vinegared rice (*shari*) #3, see page 18
2 oz.(60 g) flounder
10 leaves *sansho* or substitute other greens, such as watercress although there is no real
   alternative for the flavor of fresh *sansho* leaves in fragrance
20 leaves of camellia, washed and dried
salt and rice vinegar (*su*)

Method:
Prepare vinegared rice (*shari*). Put aside.

Cut the flounder into 10 pieces. Sprinkle lightly with salt. Set aside for 15 minutes. Rinse salt off in rice vinegar. Discard this vinegar.

Squeeze a cloth dampened with vinegar/water solution (*tezu*), see page 14. Put the fish on the cloth. Place the *sansho* on it. Lay the vinegared rice ball (approximately 2 tablespoons rice) on it. Wrap the cloth around the combination. Squeeze to shape into round balls. Remove cloth carefully.

Place the round rice ball between two camellia leaves. In place of the camellia, leaves of cherry trees and *shiso* (beefsteak plant) can be used.

Discard camellia leaves when eating.

Left: *Sushi* with
Camellia Leaves
Right: *Sushi* with Cherry
Leaves and Blossoms

KAKI-NO-HA-ZUSHI

Literally translates to *sushi* with autumn hued persimmon leaves. During the fall when the beautiful array of reds, oranges and pale greens appear on your persimmon tree, make this colorful seasonal *sushi* to feast both visually and to satisfy your craving for *sushi*. Discard the leaf wrapper prior to eating.

Ingredients:
3 cups vinegared rice (*shari*) #3, see page 18
colored leaves of Japanese persimmon tree, washed, wiped dry
smoked salmon slices (or *shime-saba* slices, see page 84)
2 eggs made into a thick omelet (sweet type), see page 23
8 shrimp, parboiled, remove veins but retain shells. Skewer and cook in boiling
    water for 2–3 minutes. Remove shells. Split shrimp carefully at back with a sharp knife.
    Soak shrimp in 2 tablespoons sugar and 2 tablespoons rice vinegar (*su*)
pickled ginger strips (either *beni-shoga* or *amazu shoga*)

Method:
Prepare vinegared rice (*shari*). Put aside.
    Slice smoked salmon or *shime-saba* thinly. Prepare egg omelet. Cut into wide strips about 1 × 2 inches (2.5 × 5 cm) long. Slice ginger into desired lengths.
    Lay the cleaned persimmon leaves flat on the palm of the left hand. Place the outer side of the leaf on the bottom and place the fish, shrimp or egg on the inner part of leaf. Then place a strip of ginger and about 1½ tablespoons of vinegared rice shaped like a long oval the width of the leaf crosswise on the leaf. See sketch.
    Roll carefully from the bottom stem end of the leaf around this filling. Place leaf rolls in alignment in a flat casserole. Cover with a lid or plate and press down with weights such as a clean brick covered with a cloth or foil to protect the food. Set aside for 2 hours or longer. This will give the *sushi* a chance to season and become firm. Eat this *sushi* by unrolling the leaf (remember to discard it) and consuming the compressed roll of *sushi* with different toppings.

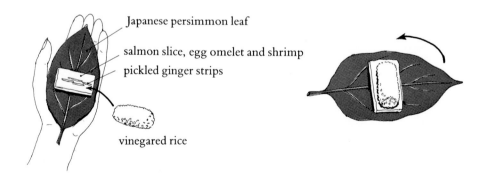

Japanese persimmon leaf

salmon slice, egg omelet and shrimp

pickled ginger strips

vinegared rice

SHAKE-ZUSHI (Salmon *Sushi*)

Ingredients:
2 cups vinegared rice (*shari*) #1, see page 18
3 large pieces of salted salmon or buy already sliced salted salmon
2 tablespoons rice vinegar for washing
2 tablespoons *saké* (Japanese rice wine)
1 tablespoon fresh ginger, slivered
a few chives, chopped

Method:
Prepare the vinegared rice (*shari*).

Freeze the salted salmon to firm up for one hour. Remove bones and skin. Slice thinly. Sprinkle salmon with the *saké*. Marinate for 15 minutes. Drain. Wash salmon with rice vinegar. Discard this vinegar.

Wipe the salmon dry with paper towels. Mix the salmon slices and slivered ginger strips with the vinegared rice mixture. Serve in bowls. Garnish with the chopped chives.

STEAMED *SUSHI* WITH SALMON

Ingredients:

2 cups vinegared rice (*shari*) #1, see page 18

2 slices salmon, broiled 15 minutes

2–3 dried *shiitake* (black Japanese forest mushrooms) soak in warm water
    20 minutes and cook as for *maki-zushi*, see page 25

7–8 slices vinegared sliced lotus root, if available (sold in small plastic
    packets). See glossary.

4–5 fresh green beans, cooked 3 minutes, sliced in 2-inch (5 cm)
    slivers on diagonal

2 eggs made into an eggsheet, see page 41

Method:

Prepare the vinegared (*shari*) rice.

Flake the broiled salmon into large pieces. Prepare mushrooms as directed. Add with the vinegared lotus root slices, string beans, slivered, to the vinegared rice (*shari*).

Cut aluminum foil into 10-inch (25 cm) squares. Divide the vinegared rice mixture into 4 equal portions. Place on the center of the foil. Bring the sides up to the center and crimp together like a pouch.

Prepare a steamer filled with about 1½ inches (3.75 cm) of water. Boil. Steam packets over high heat for 15 minutes on a rack far enough over the boiling water level so packets will not get soaked while steaming. Turn off heat. Open packet slightly and garnish top with shredded eggsheet. Serve on individual plates with the foil intact at the bottom and slightly open at the top. This is served warm.

Variation: Entire recipe could be placed in a single covered casserole to be steamed instead of in foil packets.

WAKANA-ZUSHI

This is *sushi* with *mitsuba* or watercress. *Mitsuba* is trefoil (wild Japanese chervil – Cryptotaenia japonica) and can be cultivated in your perennial vegetable or herb garden with ease. Seeds are available. Watercress, although it has a different flavor, is an acceptable substitute.

Ingredients:
2 cups vinegared rice (*shari*) #1, see page 18
½ lb.(220 g) squid mantles (cone shaped body section), cleaned, sliced in thin
    strips and parboiled in salted water for 2 minutes, drained and cooled
1 small bunch of *mitsuba* or substitute watercress
2 tablespoons toasted white sesame seeds
1 tablespoon fresh ginger
rice vinegar (*su*)

Method:
Prepare the vinegared (*shari*) rice. Put aside.

Boil *mitsuba* or watercress in boiling water for a few seconds to wilt. Sprinkle with salt. Squeeze out excess water. Chop coarsely. Chop or grind the toasted sesame seeds. Cut fresh ginger in thin 1-inch (2.5 cm) long strips.

After squid has been prepared and cooled, sprinkle with rice vinegar (*su*) and allow to stand 10 minutes. Drain. Just before serving, mix the vinegared rice with the cooked *mitsuba* or watercress, sesame seeds and half of the ginger strips.

Serve on dishes or in bowls. Top with marinated squid and ginger strips.

The picture shows trough shells (a Japanese clam) used but since this is difficult to get in America squid has been substituted in the above recipe.

SAKURA CHIRASHI

This large bowl of *chirashi* is dotted with pink so it is named *sakura* or cherry blossoms. This pink is from the pickled radish. The picture is with dried sardines but Westerners could choose fresh small bay shrimp as an excellent substitute.

Ingredients:
2 cups vinegared rice (*shari*) #1, see page 18
3½ oz.(100 g) pink colored Japanese radish (*shisozuke daikon*) sold in small packets or
    containers
½ cup dried young sardines or substitute 1 cup fresh or frozen cooked bay shrimp
    (not canned). This is sold already shelled, deveined and slightly salted usually for shrimp
    Louie salads or cocktails
1 sheet *nori* (laver seaweed) toasted one side and crumbled
2 tablespoons toasted white sesame seeds

Method:
Prepare the vinegared rice (*shari*) mixture. Put aside.
    Cook dried young sardines in boiling water until softened. Drain and put aside. Or substitute cooked bay shrimp. Chop pink colored Japanese radish. Mix the vinegared rice with the dried young sardines or the cooked bay shrimp, pink colored Japanese radishes, chopped, toasted sesame seeds and the crumbled toasted *nori*.
    Serve in bowls as shown.

SOBA-ZUSHI

Sushi does not necessarily have to be with rice as this recipe will indicate. Certain regions of Japan are known especially for tasty *soba* dishes. *Soba* (buckwheat noodles) is made with buckwheat which is rich in protein quality; high in amino acid lysine; vitamin B_6—a nutrient vital to the health of your body.

Ingredients:

2 bundles *soba* (buckwheat noodles)—comes in plastic wrapped packages
3 eggs made into a thick omelet sheet, sliced lengthwise ¼-inch (6 mm) thick julienne strips
1 bunch *mitsuba* (Japanese parsley—trefoil) parboiled 1 minute or substitute spinach, parboiled
   2 minutes
5 sheets *nori* (laver seaweed), toasted one side

Method:

Drop *soba* in plenty of boiling water over high heat. Stir to make sure noodles are distributed in the water instead of bunching up together. When water returns to boiling, add one cup of cold water. Keep over high heat and when boiling resumes again add another cup of cold water. Cook another 3–4 minutes more. Test a strand by biting into it to see if the core is cooked through. If still uncooked add another cup of cold water and repeat the cooking process . . . back to boiling and then drain thoroughly under cold running water. Allow to drain.

Spread out the *soba* on a dry clean dishcloth. The point is to have the *soba* completely dry so it can be placed on the toasted *nori* sheet without a disaster. Divide *soba* into 5 portions.

Spread a dry cloth napkin on the *sudaré* (bamboo mat). Put toasted *nori* on top of the napkin with the untoasted side uppermost. Layer the *soba* strands carefully across the *nori* leaving a ½-inch (12 mm) space at the far end of the *nori* without *soba* on it.

Place the strips of omelet in the center parallel with the *soba* layer and a line of parboiled *mitsuba* or spinach next to the egg.

Dampen the far edge of the *nori* with a drop or two of vinegar/water. Grasp the cloth covered *sudaré* closest to you and firmly roll up the *soba-zushi* away from you. Let it rest a few minutes.

Cut rolls into 1¼-inch (32 mm) widths and arrange with the cut side up as in the picture. Serve condiments of minced scallions and *wasabi* (Japanese horseradish) which are sprinkled into the following dipping sauce.

SOBA TSUYU OR SOBA-ZUYU (dipping sauce)

4 cups *dashi* (Japanese soup base)
½ cup *shoyu*
1 oz.(30 g) *katsuobushi* (bonito shavings)
Boil together for 1 minute and strain. Serve same at room temperature in individual sauce dishes.

Variations:

Warabi (bracken fern fronds), sliced bamboo shoots, *matsutake* or *shiitake* mushrooms are good seasoned for the center filling. Improvise!

KANI-ZUSHI

Kani-zushi is made with crab and other seasoned ingredients. One could substitute cooked shrimp or cooked scallops for the crab.

Ingredients:
3 cups vinegared rice (*shari*) #1, see page 18
6 dried *shiitake* (black Japanese forest mushrooms), soak in ½ cup warm water 15 minutes, squeeze out most of moisture
Mixture A:
   3 tablespoons sugar
   2 tablespoons *shoyu*
   1 tablespoon *mirin* (Japanese sweet rice wine)
2 eggs
Mixture B:
   1 teaspoon sugar
   dash salt
   1 tablespoon water
1 cup canned crabmeat or ½ lb.(220 g) freshly cooked crabmeat
Mixture C:
   2 tablespoons rice vinegar (*su*)
   1 tablespoon sugar

Method:
Prepare vinegared rice (*shari*). Put aside.

Remove *shiitake* from water. Pour off into a small pan the *shiitake* soaking liquid, being careful that the sediment is undisturbed and not used. Add *shiitake* and Mixture A. Cook together until juices are almost absorbed. Slice *shiitake* into thin strips.

Mix eggs and Mixture B. Oil a frying pan lightly. Prepare 2 thin omelets. Remove, cool and roll the sheets. Slice through roll to make thin strips.

Flake crabmeat and remove cartilages. Mix together with Mixture C.

Garnish: Pickled *beni-shoga* (red pickled ginger), cut in thin matchsticks 2 sheets *nori*, toasted and crushed into tiny pieces.

Prepare the vinegared rice (*shari*). Put this rice into a large round platter. Shape it into a neat mound. Place the crabmeat, *shiitake*, egg and crumbled *nori* in a decorative pattern on top of the rice. Garnish with the slivers of *beni-shoga*.

Variation: Combine the entire seasoned ingredients lightly folding together with the vinegared rice. Reserve some egg strips for the garnish along with the *beni-shoga* and crumbled *nori* pieces.

AVOCADO/CRAB CALIFORNIA ROLL

In California since the advent of the *sushi* bars there has been a most interesting development in *sushi*. Chefs are utilizing the very delicious ripe avocado, sliced, along with crab legs to form a dazzling "California Roll." The oil content and smooth texture of the avocado is similar to *maguro* (tuna) and combined with crab it is delicious!

There are quite a few adaptations of this idea:
* Toast *nori* sheet, cut in quarters and place on your hand. Vinegared rice (*shari*) is placed thereon. In the center a slice of avocado and a crab leg meat portion are aligned with a sprinkle of toasted white sesame seeds. This is rolled like a fat cigar.
* Another version is to place the toasted *nori* sheet cut in quarters on the *sudaré*. The avocado slice is placed thereon along with the crabmeat. This is rolled at this point with the *nori* surrounding the ingredients. Then the vinegared rice (*shari*) is formed by hand around the *nori* to produce a *nigiri-zushi*-type oval. A reverse *norimaki*! This is in turn rolled in toasted white sesame seeds.
* My favorite method is to make it buffet-style. The avocado slices sprinkled with lemon juice to prevent oxidation lined up with crab portions and a small dish of toasted sesame seeds placed on a serving platter. A bowl of vinegared rice (*shari*) made up into small balls ready to be picked up by the guests. The toasted *nori* is cut into quarters and stacked close by. And the star of the show is a bunch of fresh green *shiso* leaves ready to be included in the combination. Prepare your own *temaki-zushi*. Dip in *shoyu* to eat.
* Avocado slices can have lemon juice sprinkled on them and placed on a regular *nigiri-zushi* assortment of *tané* (toppings). Shrimp or scallops would work equally well with avocado. Or you can use avocado as a surprise filler in a *maki-zushi/hosomaki*.

Substitute for crab: A very delicious alternative to expensive crab legs is an imitation crab (*kani no kamaboko*) made from pollack, potato starch, sugar and salt with coloring and flavor of crab. This is a steamed fishcake produced in Japan and sold frozen in America. It is marvelous!

CHICKEN/PORK *GOMOKU-ZUSHI*

This *sushi* basic recipe was used in my Western cooking classes for years. It utilizes canned *gomoku-no-moto* (prepared vegetables for *sushi*) as well as fresh ingredients. The use of chicken/pork as an ingredient is an innovation for families who do not "go for" seafood. Perfect for Americans.

My students would exclaim, "Why, *sushi* is a rice salad!" And how true it is. Seasoned vinegared rice with vegetables, fish or meat, etc. With open minds "enter" this new gastronomical gourmet experience.

Ingredients:

3 cups short or medium grain rice (i.e. Kokuho or Calrose)
3 cups + 3 tablespoons water
Mixture A:
    6 tablespoons rice vinegar (*su*)
    4½ tablespoons sugar or slightly less
    2 teaspoons salt.
    dash MSG (optional)

Method:

Prepare rice and water as directed under *shari*, see page 18. Heat Mixture A in small non-metallic pan. Mix to dissolve sugar. Set aside. When the rice is cooked, toss with vinegar/water solution (*tezu*), page 14, dipped *shamoji* (rice paddle). Use a wooden bowl if available. Add heated vinegar solution to hot rice, carefully folding into rice without mashing kernels. Do this quickly. Fan constantly to cool. Use an electric fan—it will save your physical energy! Rice kernels will be quite lustrous. Mix lightly from the bottom up.

How to use the above basic seasoned rice (*shari*):

Ingredients:

6 *agé* (fried soybean cake)
Mixture B:
    ¾ cup chicken stock
    ½ cup raw chicken or lean pork meat, chopped coarsely
    2 tablespoons sugar
    2 tablespoons *shoyu*
    1 teaspoon sherry or *mirin* (sweet rice wine)
1 can (7½ oz.) *gomoku-no-moto* (prepared *sushi* vegetables)
¼ cup thawed frozen green peas
½ small carrot, coarsely shredded (optional)

Method:

Cut *agé* crosswise in half, carefully split center portion and make pocket. Place in colander. Run boiling water over *agé* until a lot of oiliness is washed away. Put in large pan and add lots of water. Boil and drain. Squeeze out excess water carefully. Put aside.

Simmer Mixture B for 5 minutes to cook the raw meat, then place the "degreased" *agé* above the prepared stock mixture in pan. Place a small saucer on top of *agé* so the juices will be absorbed by the *agé* as you continue cooking. Turn over the *agé* after about 5 minutes of cooking time. Cook altogether about 10 minutes in this flavored stock. Watch carefully so pan contents will not burn. Remove *agé* onto a plate. Handle *agé* with care. Put aside.

Add canned *gomoku-no-moto* to the remaining juice/meat mixture from cooking the *agé*. Add peas and carrots for vibrant color. Adjust seasonings—you may wish more *shoyu* and sugar. Heat through. Add the prepared vegetables and meat mixture to the vinegared rice, leaving some of the juice out if too much. Mix carefully from the bottom to the top using a vinegared dampened rice paddle. This rice mixture with vegetables and meat can be served on a large platter or in individual bowls (wiped first with vinegar/water solution, see page 14, so *sushi* will not stick). It would be called *gomoku-zushi* at this point. Garnish with thin strips of egg omelet, toasted *nori* (laver seaweed) and *beni-shoga* (pickled red ginger). *(Continued on page 122)*

INARI-ZUSHI (Cooked seasoned *agé* filled with flavored rice)

(Continued from page 121)
The prepared vegetables/meat mixture and *shari* become the filling. Fill *agé* lightly and carefully. Do not pack. Tuck the bottom edges of the *agé* under so the filling will not all spill out. Stand the filled *agé* with the cut portion at the bottom. This 3 cups of rice/vegetables/meat mixture will fill the 12 half-cut *agé* and leave you enough to serve the balance on a platter for *gomoku-zushi*.

Variations and hints:

* The vinegared rice (*shari*) alone can be mixed with toasted black or white sesame seeds and used as a filling for the prepared *agé*.
* The prepared *agé* can be chopped and added with the vegetables and meat to the vinegared rice to make a *gomoku-zushi*.
* If you desire to prepare this vegetables/meat combination without the *agé*, reduce the stock to ⅓ cup and proceed to simmer meat 10 minutes and add the *gomoku-no-moto*. Add peas for color. Heat thoroughly. Add to vinegared rice, draining off extra juices if there is too much liquid.
* If you wish to make your own vegetable combination, shred some carrots, fresh string beans, burdock (*gobo*), lotus root, *shiitake*, bamboo shoots, etc. and flavor by adding more *shoyu* and sugar to your taste.
* The canned type of prepared *sushi* vegetables by cooking together with the meat and stock loses the "canned tin taste."
* I do not suggest using canned *agé*. It is very thin and dry and I feel it just does not have the true tenderness and texture of fresh *agé*. But, again, if you cannot locate fresh or frozen *agé*, use it. It can be "revived" flavorwise by cooking in flavored juices of vegetables/meat.
* These *sushi* variations make excellent picnic fare. They are at their best when made hours before serving. *Sushi* should not be refrigerated except in a dire emergency. *Sushi* is highly perishable. This is the reaction of the acid on the starches. Keep in a cool place covered with foil.
* Give the *sushi* a chance to cool down to room temperature so you can get the true flavor after it has penetrated each kernel of rice.
* Bits of cerise red *beni-shoga* go well with *sushi*. The salty, pungent flavor just hits the spot. Cut matchstick slivered pieces and use as a garnish to be eaten.
* Often a garnish of shrimp called *oboro* is used. To prepare use a 5 oz.(150 g) can of shrimp. Wash, drain and mash shrimp. Place in a small hot frying pan. Add a few drops of red food coloring to 2 teaspoons sugar and mix with shrimp. Cook over low heat until shrimp meat is flaky and dry.

SPECIAL TEA
AND
SOUPS
FOR *SUSHI*

JAPANESE TEA (*o-cha*)

Sencha (a medium grade of green tea) or *Bancha* (the least expensive coarse green tea) is good to drink along with *sushi*.
Gyokuro (the most refined green tea and expensive too) is not suited.

Method of preparation: Pour hot water into the ceramic tea pot to heat it. Discard. The tea leaves are then put into the pot and very hot water poured on the *sencha* leaves and allowed to steep for 2–3 minutes. For *bancha* use boiling hot water. Do not use too many tea leaves. Just enough to yield an amber colored liquid to be served with no cream or sugar . . . just plain to complement the *sushi* flavors. You will agree that hot green tea is true ambrosia savored in the large tall tea cups with *sushi*.

Suimono (Japanese Clear Soups)

Note that the soup bowls have been arranged artistically in preparation for the hot clear broth which will be poured carefully in order not to disturb the "picture design." Then the lids are placed on the bowls to keep the soup hot.

1
Sea bream,
Fu (Wheat gluten bread) and
Shungiku (Chrysanthemum leaves)

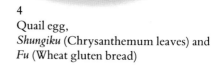

4
Quail egg,
Shungiku (Chrysanthemum leaves) and
Fu (Wheat gluten bread)

2
Kamaboko (Steamed fishcake) and
Mitsuba (Trefoil)

5
Seaweed and
Kinomé

3
Kamaboko (Steamed fishcake),
Mitsuba (Trefoil) and
Lemon peel

6
Mung bean threads or Harusame,
Fu (Wheat gluten bread) and
Green beans

7
Tofu (Soybean cake) and
Chives

8
Omelet,
Fu (Wheat gluten bread) and
Green beans

9
Kamaboko (Steamed fishcake),
Fresh *shiitake* and
Snow peas

10
Canned crabmeat,
Mitsuba (Trefoil) and
Nori (Laver seaweed)

BASIC *SUIMONO* (Clear Japanese Soup)

Suimono literally means something to drink. The Japanese clear soups are an aesthetic picture in themselves as you can well see by the pictures. Very simple and yet very sophisticated in their presentation. The flavor is exquisite as compared to some other ethnic type soups. Do not sloppily ladle the soup into attractive bowls. Be artistic! Use covered lacquered Japanese bowls if you have them. The serving becomes so much more authentic and the soup retains the heat well. When one uncovers the lid the visual soup picture is beautiful!

BASIC *DASHI* (Stock—for clear soup and for cooking)

Japanese clear soups have no fat and good stock is very crystal clear. There is a certain exquisite, sparkling, sweet, subtle flavor and aroma from the products of the sea—*kombu* (kelp) and *katsuo* (bonito fish flakes) combine to impart a characteristic sweetness to *suimono*.

Fill a pot with 4½ cups cold water. Add an 8-inch (20 cm) square piece of dried *dashi kombu* (kelp for soup). When the water comes to a boil remove the *kombu*. Add the ½ cup *katsuo* (dried bonito fish flakes). Immediately remove pot from the heat source. The fish flakes will sink to the bottom of the pan. Strain in a colander lined with cheesecloth.

Season with 1 to 1½ teaspoons salt, a dash of *saké* (Japanese rice wine) to the broth. If desired a few drops of *shoyu* (only Japanese soy sauce is suitable) can be added at the very last. Taste as you season to keep the flavor very light and delicate.

Valuable hints: If this stock preparation is cooked too long the *kombu* results in a cloudy and bitter *dashi*. Time is of essence. One could substitute instant *dashi* powder which is not as exquisite but very passable. And we all have those days of need for quick instant options. Chicken broth could be used but it will not be quite the desired Japanese taste. But again we in the West are adaptable and we blend many combinations to develop those tastes that will suit our families best. However try to make *dashi* at least once . . . it is worth it . . . after all this is a book on *sushi* and feasting on the authentic with the complementing recipes will yield you the greatest gourmet dazzling tastes—or "*aji*" as the Japanese word for flavor signifies.

Variations for clear soup which go especially well with *sushi* dishes *See pages 126–127.*
1. Sliced sea bream which is first poached in hot water briefly. Wheat gluten bread (*fu*) and edible chrysanthemum leaves (*shungiku*).
2. Red and white *kamaboko* (steamed fishcake) blanched briefly to heat through. Tied trefoils (*mitsuba*) for garnish.
3. *Kamaboko* (steamed fishcake), tied trefoil (*mitsuba*) and slivered citron or lemon peel.
4. Quail egg (canned), hot water poured over the egg prior to use. Edible chrysanthemum leaves (*shungiku*) and wheat gluten bread (*fu*).
5. Seaweed, *kinomé* (Japanese pepper plant), chopped and garnished with a leaf of bamboo.
6. Bean thread sticks (mung bean threads) or *harusamé* (Japanese yam threads) cooked in boiling water until translucent, wheat gluten bread (*fu*) with cooked green beans, sliced, for garnish.
7. Soybean curd (*tofu*) diced with chives cut in 1-inch (2.5 cm) lengths.
8. Omelet (cut in triangular shape), wheat gluten bread (*fu*) and cooked green beans, sliced thin.
9. *Kamaboko* (steamed fishcake), sliced, fresh *shiitake* (black Japanese mushrooms) or button mushrooms (cooked in soup for 1 minute) with cooked green snow peas for garnish.
10. Canned crabmeat, trefoil (*mitsuba*) and *nori* (laver seaweed), sliced in thin strips.

Procedure: Use the basic 4 cups *dashi* which has been strained, heated and seasoned. Place the assorted desired ingredients into soup bowls. Carefully pour the hot soup therein. Do not destroy the aesthetic image you have "arranged" in the bowl. You desire the steaming aroma to entice the diner when the cover is opened as well as your "picture soup" to receive compliments. Use your imagination in the design preparation of your sparkling *suimono*.

SPECIAL *SUIMONO*

These soups are all very light and will enhance as well as complement the rich flavors of *sushi*.

■ CLEAR SOUP WITH CLAMS

Ingredients:
8 fresh clams
4 rape or mustard blossoms or watercress
4 cups water
1½ teaspoons salt or less
1 tablespoon *mirin* (Japanese sweet rice wine)
4 leaves of *kinomé* (Japanese pepper plant—*sansho*)

Method:
Cook rape blossoms, mustard or watercress in boiling water for 1 minute. Rinse in cold water. Drain.

Choose fresh clams which have a good solid sound when they are tapped. Put scrubbed clams in 4 cups water. Bring to a boil. Remove the meat from the clams one by one. Put aside. Add salt and *mirin* to remaining soup that you cooked the clams in. Heat. Fill both sides of the opened shells with the clam meat. Discard the extra 4 clam shells from which meat had been removed. Place carefully in bowls. Lay the rape blossoms (or mustard or watercress) on top of clams. Pour the soup carefully. Float the *kinomé* on top.

■ CLEAR SOUP WITH SEA URCHIN AND ABALONE

Ingredients:
sea urchin, if available, enough for 4 soup servings
1 abalone slice 4 × 4 inches (10 × 10 cm) or substitute fresh squid mantles,
    cut either one in strips
4 green vegetable leaves such as spinach
4 leaves of *kinomé* (Japanese pepper plant—*sansho*) or substitute *mitsuba*
    or watercress sprig
4 cups soup base prepared from instant dashi mixture if you do not have
    home–made *dashi* made from scratch
salt to taste
½ tablespoon saké (Japanese rice wine)
dash *shoyu*

Method:

Fill pot with soup base. Bring to a boil. Season with salt, *saké* and a dash of *shoyu*. (If prepared with instant *dashi* mixture it is already salted—therefore taste first). Add sea urchin and sliced abalone or squid. Turn off the heat source. Put the sea urchin and abalone or squid and the soup into each bowl. Float a green vegetable and sprig of *kinomé* on top. The sea urchin when cooked appears like a strawberry.

■ CLEAR SOUP WITH SHRIMP

Ingredients:

4 medium-size shrimp, shelled but with tails left intact; veins removed
cornstarch
1 fresh string bean, sliced thinly on diagonal or use other vegetable such as carrot, etc.
4 sprigs of *kinomé* (Japanese pepper plant—*sansho*) or substitute watercress
4 cups soup base (*dashi*)
salt, *saké* and a dash of *shoyu*

Method:

Slightly salt the raw shrimp. Dip in cornstarch. Parboil 2 minutes in boiling water. Boil string bean for 1 minute in boiling water. Heat the soup base. Taste and if necessary flavor lightly with salt and *saké*. Add *shoyu* at the very last only if needed.

Put 1 cooked shrimp in each bowl with the string bean slices on top. Pour soup carefully over the shrimp. Garnish with *kinomé*.

In each of these soup recipes you will note that *kinomé* is used to decorate the soup serving. One can use a piece of watercress or a sliver of lemon rind. You do not necessarily have to use *kinomé* although it would be truly Japanese if you could get some.

This *sansho* plant grows in a most satisfactory manner in a partially shaded place. It is known as prickly ash (zanthoxylum piperatum) and is available at certain specialty nurseries.

■ CLEAR SOUP WITH PINK WHEAT GLUTEN BREAD (*FU*)

Ingredients:

1 fillet of sole or other delicate white fleshed fish such as seabass
1 thin egg omelet, sliced in long thin strips
4 wheat gluten bread (*fu*), pink color
a few sprigs of *mizuna* (a Japanese mustard variety) or substitute spinach
4 sprigs *kinomé* (Japanese pepper plant-*sansho*)
5 cups soup base prepared from instant *dashi* mixture if you do not have *dashi* made from scratch
salt and *saké* (Japanese rice wine)

Method:

Cut the fish slantwise into 4 pieces. Sprinkle with salt. Roll into a circle and fasten each piece with toothpicks. Put aside. Blanch the *mizuna* or spinach in boiling water for 1 minute. Slice. Cook wheat gluten bread in 1 cup of seasoned soup briefly to expand. Heat 4 cups soup base. Taste and if necessary season with salt and *saké* for a light flavor. Add the fish and cook for 2 minutes.

Place fish with the toothpicks removed in soup bowls. Add the pink wheat gluten bread, *mizuna* or spinach and pour in the soup carefully. Garnish with the *kinomé*.

Clear soup with clams

Clear soup with shrimp

Clear soup with sea urchin and abalone

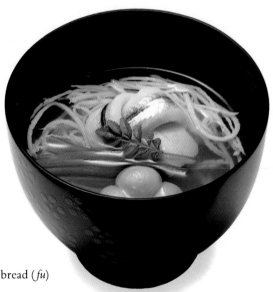

Clear soup with pink wheat gluten bread (*fu*)

HOW TO SELECT FRESH FISH

How does one know a fresh fish? Fresh fish should have flesh very firm and spring back when pressed upon gently; should have clear shiny eyes; not cloudy; should have shiny skin. The "fragrance" of fresh fish is mild; not a bit of fishy odor. As fillets the flesh should be moist, appear freshly cut and glossy; not looking dried out and brownish on edges or drab. Fish is very perishable and should be refrigerated at 35°–40°F. (1.6°–4.4°C.) immediately.

It should be used that day, if possible. There is also a seasonal time to enjoy fish for the peak in flavor.

Body

Fresh

Not fresh

Fresh
Firm, odorless

Not fresh
Dull, drab color

Scales

Fresh

Not fresh

Fresh
Firmly attached

Not fresh
Loosely attached

Gills

Fresh
Bright red, fresh odor

Not fresh
Dark red, smelly

Fresh

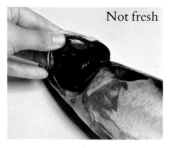
Not fresh

Eyes

Fresh

Not fresh

Fresh
Bright

Not fresh
Dull

132

DIFFERENT KINDS OF ROE

The introduction of *sushi* to those outside of Japan has brought on a gourmet taste for salmon, flying fish, crab and cod roes as never before. Therefore the availability of more and more types of roe either fresh or frozen has widened. True caviar has always been a luxury item but now instead of sturgeon eggs only, caviar is being made from other sources.

The eggs are separated from the connecting membranes and firmed with salt or special brines. There are many colors and textures of unusual fish roes on the market.

All of these are delicious used on top of *sushi* rice. Try making a "battleship-shaped" *gunkanmaki zushi*, see page 96, with a scoop of sparkling beads of roe. There is fabulous flavor—each bite bursts open the wee eggs. One can be dramatic by using three different colored roes for a tri-color effect.

Here are three very popular *sushi* topping roes:

Masago: Crab roe has a delicate crunch with a bittersweet flavor. Lightly colored pale orange.

Tobiko shiozuke: Flying fish roe has a bit of fishy flavor with very crunchy texture. Deeply colored dark orange-brown.

Ajitsuke tarako: Cod roe is flesh colored and the loose salted eggs are similar to anchovy paste. This comes from Japan and some from Canada.

To eliminate the excess salt, the coloring material, fishiness and preservative taste rinse in a very fine mesh strainer so the eggs will not slip through the holes. Allow cold water to pass through a few minutes. Drain well and refrigerate until cold before using as a topping for *sushi*. The above are only a few suggested roes. Your fish or Asian supply foodstore will have other choices. Again imagination and daring should be the decision maker. Try!

FISH AND SHELLFISH FOR *SUSHI*

Which can be served raw and which should be cooked? Here are some suggestions:
abalone (raw)
aoyagi (raw)
ark shell (raw)
clam (raw)
crab (cooked)
flatfish (raw)
roe (raw) or salted
sea bass (raw)
sea bream (raw)
sea urchin (see roe)
tuna (raw)
conger eel (cooked)
mackerel (marinated raw)
octopus (cooked)
salmon (salted) although some eat raw
shrimp (cooked) although true gourmets delight in eating the live "*odori*" (dancing) shrimp
squid (raw and cooked)

A KALEIDOSCOPE OF FISH AND SHELLFISH IN AMERICA

This list is very general. No attempt has been made to put in all regional fish names, types or varieties. It would be an impossible task since there is quite an overlap of fish types in different localities. Availability depends on weather conditions, changes in ocean currents, etc. Seek the helping hand of your experienced fish market to make your choice. For *sushi* salt water fish is the safest and wisest to use. Otherwise cook it first.

Salt water Types/Varieties	When available	Where caught
Albacore, Pacific Yellow fin, skipjack	summer July–Oct.	Western coast Northwestern coast
Bluefish blue snapper, skipjack, snapping mackerel	all year	Eastern, Gulf coasts
Bonito sea tuna, skipjack tuna	July–Oct. frozen available	Southwestern, Mid-eastern, Western coasts
Cod, Atlantic or Pacific codfish	all year frozen available	Northeastern, Mid-eastern, Western coasts
Croaker white sea bass, corvina, Atlantic croaker	March–Oct. esp. summer/autumn	Mid-eastern, Southern coasts
Eel American eel, Moray, Conger, silver eel	best in autumn frozen available	Eastern coast
Flounder or sole (Flatfish) petrale sole, Dover sole, rex sole, English sole, turbot, blackback flounder, winter and summer flounder	all year	Northeastern, Mideastern, Western coasts
Grouper sea bass	Nov.–May	Southeastern, Pacific coasts, Gulf of Mexico

Haddcock (related to cod) scrod	all year frozen available	Northeastern coast
Halibut, Pacific	May–Sept. frozen available	Western coast
Herring, Pacific herring roe	Jan.–Feb. frozen available	Pacific coast
Herring, Atlantic sea herring	Winter through late spring	Northeastern, Mid-eastern, Western coasts
Mackerel Boston mackerel, Spanish mackerel, Atlantic mack- erel, Pacific mackerel, American mackerel, horse mackerel	all year, spring and summer in Eastern areas	Northeastern, Mid-eastern, Western coasts. Frozen from Japan
Ocean perch, Atlantic	all year frozen available	Northeastern coast
Porgy white snapper, sea bream, northern porgy, scup	Sept.–May especially good Jan.–April	Eastern coast
Rock fish rock cod, sea bass, grouper, red snapper ocean perch, rosefish	all year	Western coast
Sable fish black cod, Alaska cod	all year, best in summer in Calif. Aug.–Nov. in North- west	Western coast
Salmon chinook, silver sockeye salmon, pink salmon, Atlantic salmon	summer and fall frozen available	Northeastern, Western coasts
Sea Bass black sea bass, white sea bass, striped bass, blackfish	all year	Western, Eastern coasts

Shad and Roe	March–May frozen roe available	Eastern, Northwestern coasts
Shark	all year, especially summer	Western, Southeastern and Gulf coasts
Smelt	all year	Gulf, Western and Eastern coasts
Snapper, Red good substitute for sea bream	all year	Gulf, Western and Eastern coasts
Striped bass rockfish striper	all year, summer good	Mideastern, Southeastern, Southern Calif. coasts
Swordfish	Aug.–Oct. frozen available	Northeastern, Mideastern, Eastern and Western coasts
Tuna	all year, Autumn best frozen available	Pacific/Hawaii
Yellowtail California	all year	Pacific, Mexico
Roes, preserved	frozen available	Imported and domestic
Abalone	fresh and frozen	Western coast and imported
Clams geoduck, King clam, gooey-duck, ark shell	seasonal frozen available	Northwestern, Eastern coasts. Imported
Hard Clams little neck, cherrystone clam	seasonal	Eastern coast
Crab stone, rock and blue crabs	seasonal frozen available	Eastern and Gulf coasts
Dungeness crab	Nov.–July frozen available	Western coast, Alaska
Alaskan King crab	frozen available	Alaska

Lobster		
northern Maine lobster	Oct.–May	Eastern coast
Spring Pacific lobster, rock lobster	frozen tails year round	Southwestern, Mexico coasts
Octopus		
polpi, devilfish	fresh all year frozen available	Western coast frozen frozen imported
Oysters	seasonal	Eastern, Northwestern and Western coasts
Scallops		
bay scallops	all year and frozen	Eastern, Gulf coasts
sea scallops, fan shell	all year and frozen	Eastern coasts
Sea Urchin		
roe	spring summer, autumn, winter frozen imported available	Eastern coast Pacific coast
Shrimp		
prawn, ocean shrimp, bay shrimp, northern shrimp, Alaskan shrimp	all year frozen available	Northern, Southeastern, Gulf, Western coasts
Squid		
calamari	fresh June–Aug. frozen available	Northeastern, Mideastern, Western coasts

GLOSSARY

Aburagé: See *Agé*

Agari: Japanese green tea term used at a *sushi* bar—usually *o-agari*.

Agé: Deep-fried soybean cake (*tofu*); a short term for *aburagé*

Agé-zushi: *Sushi* made with seasoned *agé* (same as *inari-zushi*, *kitsuné-zushi*, *oinari-zushi*). Some Americanized names are cone *sushi*, footballs, rice pouches, rice sacks, *tofu* bags, treasure bags and certainly you will be coming up with your special name!

Aji: Spanish mackerel, horse mackerel

Akagai: A Japanese clam variety

Akami: Red flesh of tuna fillet

Anago: Conger eel, a long salt water fish for *sushi* broiled with a thick sweet sauce brushed on it.

Anakyu: Small *maki-zushi* with cooked *anago* and sliced cucumber strip in center

Aoyagi: A Japanese clam variety. The reddish foot portion is used raw.

Atsuyaki tamago: A thick Japanese-style sweet omelet, rolled, then sliced.

Awabi: Abalone

Battéra: *Sushi* made by pressing in a mold with marinated mackerel topping. This could also be called *oshi-zushi*.

Beni-shoga: Red salted pickled ginger root used for garnish as well as a condiment with *sushi*.

Chirashi: Served in a lacquered bowl with *sushi* rice at the bottom and assorted ingredients placed attractively on top or the *chirashi* can be served on a large platter or bowl.

Chirashi-zushi: *Sushi* rice and flavored ingredients combined together. Also called *gomoku-zushi*, *gomoku-meshi* or *maze gohan*. Often these varied names depend upon certain regions in Japan. Can be served on a large platter or bowl with attractive garnishes on top, i.e. shrimp, *kinomé*, etc.

Chumaki: See *Futomaki*

Chutoro: Tuna—the fatty pale pink portion.

Daikon: White Japanese long radish. *Daikon* has very choice enzymes which help digest starches such as rice.

Dashi: Japanese stock prepared with kelp and dried bonito (*katsuobushi*).

Ebi: Shrimp

Edomae: Tokyo-style *sushi*—Edo being the ancient name for Tokyo.

Engawa: Chewy halibut flesh by the fins

Funamori: *Sushi* rice shaped like a miniature boat with toasted *nori* wrapped around the oval and a mound of topping. Also called *gunkan maki*.

Fu: Gluten bread made into dehydrated pieces—often colored pink and green. Used in soups.

Futomaki: A fat version of *maki-zushi*/ *norimaki*. A rolled *sushi* with a center of different seasoned ingredients.

Gari: Rice vinegar seasoned ginger. This term used only at a *sushi* bar.

Goma: Sesame seeds—used toasted in *sushi* making.

Gomoku-zushi: See *Chirashi-zushi*.

Gyoku: See *atsuyaki tamago*. This term used only at a *sushi* bar.

Hamachi:	A mackerel type
Hamaguri:	A Japanese clam variety
Hibarigai:	A Japanese clam variety
Hiramé:	Like a sole, flat fish
Himo:	The stringy portion of *akagai* clam
Himokyu:	A small *makizushi* with *himo* and cucumber in center.
Ika:	Squid. In Japan could be *koika* or *mongoika* depending upon size and variety.
Ikura:	Salmon eggs (roe)—caviar
Inari:	See *agé-zushi*
Inari-zushi:	See *agé-zushi*
Ise-ebi no arai:	*Sashimi* made from live lobster
Itamae:	*Sushi* chef
Kai:	A clam
Kani:	Crab
Kampyo:	Dried shaved strips of a Japanese vegetable that belongs to the *yugao* family (bottle calabash).
Kansai-zushi:	*Osaka* (western Japan) style *sushi*
Kanto:	*Tokyo* (eastern Japan). In ancient days called *Edo* area.
Kazunoko:	Herring eggs
Kohada:	A Japanese fish marinated similar to a sardine with silvery skin and used for topping of *nigiri-zushi*.
Kombu:	Kelp sea vegetable used for *dashi* preparation
Koyadofu:	Soybean cake which has been frozen and then dehydrated
Maguro:	Tuna
Maki-zushi:	Rolled *sushi* with *nori* on the outside and assorted seasoned egg/vegetables/fish in the center . . . of average rolled size. Variation see *Futomaki*. Could be called *norimaki*.
Masago:	Crab roe
Maze gohan:	See *chirashi-zushi*
Mirin:	Sweet wine made from glutinous rice for cooking purposes.
Mirugai:	Japanese clam with a long siphon-type neck similar to American geoduck or horseneck clam.
Nare-zushi:	Fermented *sushi*
Neta:	Ingredients for *sushi*
Nigiri-zushi:	Hand formed oval shaped *sushi* with assorted toppings.
Nori:	Laver seaweed (sea vegetable) in flat sheets approximately 8 by 9-inches(20×22.5 cm). The ideal and best is *Asakusa Nori*. Toast outside prior to use to bring out crispness, good aroma, flavor and color.
Norimaki:	See *maki-zushi*
Ohyo:	Halibut
Oinari:	See *agézushi*
Oshibori:	Hot steaming small towels (colder days) and refreshingly cold small towels (hotter days), rolled and "served" to you for wiping hands prior to eating. A special hint: To prepare *o-shibori* towels . . . dampen and squeeze excess water from small face towels. Roll tightly and place on pyrex pie dish. Cover with plastic wrap. Place in microwave for 1–2 minutes. You will get excellent "hot" results for serving to guests. Be careful that they do not steam burn themselves.
Oshi-zushi:	Pressed *sushi* Osaka style
Otsumami:	Appetizer tid-bits that go well with *sushi* and drinks such as *sashimi*, grilled shrimps, etc.
Saba:	Mackerel
Saba-zushi:	*Sushi* rice topped with marinated mackerel and pressed down in a form.

139

Sabi:	*Wasabi*, Japanese horseradish —used in *sushi* shop terminology.
Sabi nuki:	Without any *wasabi*—used in *sushi* shop terminology.
Saké:	Japanese rice wine—usually warmed for serving.
Sashimi:	Freshly sliced raw fish fillets.
Shari:	Short grain rice steamed and seasoned with rice vinegar, sugar and salt for *sushi* preparation. This is the basic rice for *sushi* making.
Shako:	Mantis shrimp grey-colored, from shallow ocean waters.
Shiitake:	Japanese black forest mushrooms—dried ones used for preparing *sushi* since the flavor is intense and excellent.
Shimesaba:	Marinated mackerel.
Shiso:	Japanese herb (perilla frutcscens) or commonly known as beefsteak plant with a very definite flavor; two varieties —green and reddish purple leaves. The little flower spikes are also relished for their crunchy distinct touch.
Shoga:	Ginger root—available fresh in States but the quality is not consistent—sometimes flesh is fibrous and dried out. In Japan very tender shoots and roots available. Substitute preserved varieties to serve with *sushi*.
Shoyu:	Japanese soy sauce. Very light and flavorful. Do not substitute Chinese or other soy sauce—the *sushi* flavor will be disastrous since other types of soy sauce often have molasses added and are denser.
Su:	Japanese rice vinegar made from glutinous rice. The only kind of vinegar suitable for *sushi* making. White distilled vinegar could be diluted with water but it would not have the sweet flavor of the Japanese *su*.
Sudaré:	Like a bamboo place mat. Bamboo thin skewers woven together with string and used as a rolling mat for certain types of *sushi*.
Sugata-zushi:	When the fish in its complete form, head and tail, is used this pressed *sushi* is called *sugata zushi*.
Suribachi:	Japanese ceramic mortar.
Sushi ya:	Restaurant specializing in *sushi*.
Suzuko:	Fish roe
Tai:	Japanese fish often termed sea bream or red snapper.
Taira-gai:	Scallops
Tako:	Octopus
Takuan:	Pickled yellow *daikon* radish
Tané:	Topping ingredients used for *nigiri-zushi*.
Tekka-maki:	Small *maki-zushi/norimaki* rolled *maguro* (tuna) in center.
Temaki:	Miniature *maki-zushi/norimaki* rolled by hand instead of on a *sudaré*.
Teppo-maki:	Small *maki-zushi/norimaki* with *kanpyo* in center.
Torigai:	A dark colored and chewy clam available in America frozen from Japan.
Toro:	Oily part of tuna fillet (light, pinkish)
Tsumami:	Same as *otsumami*.
Unagi:	Eel
Uni:	Sea urchin roe
Wasabi:	Japanese green colored horseradish. See *Sabi*. Fresh is expensive so use canned powdered *wasabi* and mix with water.

INDEX OF RECIPES

Italicized numbers designate illustrations

OSHI-ZUSHI (Molded and Pressed *Sushi*)

Molded Ham-*Zushi*	82,*83*
Oshi-Zushi	
with Conger Eel and Cucumber	79,80
with Flounder and *Kinomé*	78,*79*
with Salmon and *Nori*, Hakata-Style	79,80
with Shrimp and rolled Omelet	79,80

SPECIAL TEA AND *MINI-ZUSHI*

Japanese Tea	*125*
Mini-Mini-*Zushi*	94,*95*

STUFFED AND FOLDED *SUSHI*

Inari-Zushi	
Inari-Zushi	60,*61*
Kitsune-Zushi	62,*63*
Inari-Zushi	122,*123*
Sushi in Omelet Sheets	
Chakin-Zushi	57,*58*
Fukusa-Zushi	56,*59*
Hamaguri-Zushi	57,*59*

SUIMONO

Basic *Suimono* (Clear Japanese Soup)	*126,127*,128
Basic *Dashi*/10 Variations for Clear Soup	*126,127*,128
Special *Suimono*	
Clear Soup with Clams	129,*131*
Clear Soup with Pink Wheat Gluten Bread	130,*131*
Clear Soup with Sea Urchin and Abalone	129,*131*
Clear Soup with Shrimp	130,*131*